A Choice Fulfilled

A Choice Fulfilled
The Business of High Technology

by
Charles K. Kao

The Chinese University Press

ISBN 962–201–521–2

THE CHINESE UNIVERSITY PRESS
The Chinese University of Hong Kong
SHATIN, N.T., HONG KONG

Printed in Hong Kong by Turbo Printing Co., Ltd.

Contents

Preface

My one time colleague in British industry, turned academic professor, and now rector of a famous university coaxed me at all his lectures on highly technical topics, to believe every word that he uttered. Yet every time I tried to convince my audiences that technology had changed our business world, specifically high tech business, no one appeared to be convinced.

Several years ago when I was working in Germany, I took a deep breath one day and wrote the gist of my arguments down. I decided that if I expanded the salient points in full, I should be able to demonstrate unequivocally my convictions. During that hot summer, when all the Germans were on vacation, I roughed out my first draft. Since then I have had the chance to reflect on the subject and to add a couple of chapters.

According to me, this manuscript, when edited into a book, should become a best seller! Much facts are given for the reader to reflect upon, some self-evident and some thought-provoking. The return on investment in buying this volume is very high. The book is organized for fast reading for those who would like to just get a feel, but it is really for readers to browse through and then to think about the many points raised on almost every page. This book, though geared for a person with a science or engineering background, has business pointers that would apply to any high tech market.

A look at the titles of the chapters might convince the readers that much of the book is about technology and not too much about business. This is true. However, the first chapter, "Opportunity Un-limited," reveals the exciting vista of the new brave world in which technology has wreaked havoc and has turned the high tech business world seemingly upside down. Chapter 9 brings us into tantalizingly almost real participation in a conference on "Technology Transfer." Questions might spring to mind which the reader jumps to his feet in frustration to ask and may well find answered on the next pages. The rest of the chapters are individual examples to illustrate the causes and effects of technology on business. The transistor miracle, the computer revolution, the optical magic and the information age are all there. The multiple impacts of technology are highly revealing; a new business world with an over-abundance of opportunities, ready for any choice to be fulfilled, is awaiting.

I wish to acknowledge all those who have crossed my life and from whom I have learned. The words here are but a reflection of my experiences. In particular, I am greatly indebted to Professor and Mrs. John Espy of U.S.A. for editing the text and suggesting the addition of the two chapters, "Technology Transfer" and "The Third World." They are both retired and living in Kansas after spending over twenty years with The Chinese University of Hong Kong. John retired as a professor of international business.

Without my wife's preliminary editing and constant advice for terse and direct writing, and without her cartoon embellishments, this book would not be as appealing and readable. I would also like to acknowledge the great work done by a number of secretaries: Fraulein Blickle who typed the first manuscript from my atrocious handwriting and others who toiled through the many transcriptions.

In a recent visit to a Japanese automobile manufacturing plant, I was most happy to note the similarity of the actual tour that took place to the fictitious scene described in the opening chapter written more than five years ago. During the intervening time, I was able to consolidate my ideas while observing how the business trend moved closer to my market model. I am indebted to my colleagues and friends with whom we had a lot of interaction and from whom I received a lot of encouragement for getting the manuscript readied for publication.

Abbreviations

1-D	one-dimensional
2-D	two-dimensional
3-D	three-dimensional
ABC	American Broadcasting Corporation
AC	alternating current
AI	artificial intelligence
ASIC	Application Specific Integrated Circuit
CAD	computer-aided design
CBS	Columbia Broadcasting Service
CEO	Chief Executive Officer
COBOL	Common Business Oriented Language (a computer language for business applications)
CPU	central processing unit
CRT	cathode ray tube
DDT	dichloro-diphenyl-trichloro-ethane (an insecticide)
FAX	facsimile transmission equipment
FM	frequency modulation
FORTRAN	Formula Translator (a computer language for general and scientific applications)
GaAsP	gallium arsenide phosphide (a compound semi-conductor material)
Gb/s	gigabits/sec (10^9 b/s)
GE	General Electric Company
GHz	giga-Hertz (10^9 Hz)
GNP	Gross National Product
HDTV	high-definition television

IBM	International Business Machines
IC	integrated circuit
InGaAsP	indium gallium arsenide phosphide
INS	Information Network Systems
IRRI	International Rice Research Institute
ISDN	Integrated Services Digital Network
kb/s	kilobits/sec (10^3 b/s)
LAN	Local Area Network
LED	light-emitting diode
LISP	List Processing (a computer language for artificial intelligence applications)
LSI	large-scale integration
Mb/s	megabits/sec (10^6 b/s)
MBA	Master of Business Administration
MBE	Molecular Beam Epitaxy
MHz	mega-Hertz (10^6 Hz)
MIP	million instructions per second
MOCVD	Metallorganic Chemical Vapor Deposition
MOS	metal-oxide-silicon
MRI	Magnetic Resonance Imaging
MSI	medium-scale integration
NBC	National Broadcasting Corporation
NMR	nuclear magnetic resonance
NSF	National Science Foundation
OEM	original equipment market
OM	organization and methods
OPEC	Organization of Petroleum Exporting Countries
PBX	private branch exchange
PC	personal computer
PCM	Pulse Code Modulation
PVC	polyvinyl chloride
R&D	Research and Development
RAM	Random Access Memories
RD&E	Research, Development and Engineering

ROI	Return on Investment
TFPG	total factor productivity growth
TV	television
ULSI	ultra-large-scale integration
VCR	video tape recorder
VLSI	very-large-scale integration
WSI	wafer-scale integration

Chapter 1

Opportunities Unlimited

Br ..., Br ..., the telephone at the bedside rings. The guest in the plush room of an international business class hotel picks up the phone. He hears the computer voice saying mechanically: "This is your 7 o'clock wake-up call. A very good morning to you. The outside temperature ..." He replaces the phone and switches on his TV and tosses and turns a bit to wake himself. At 7:30 he places a phone call to his secretary to give her several messages which he could not send through the electronic mail system from his portable personal computer. "It is such a nuisance that not all hotels have the electronic mail connections," he says passionately. "Next time don't book me into just any hotel," he adds indignantly.

This scene illustrates clearly several customer needs and market opportunities fulfilled and not fulfilled. It is just a tip of an iceberg representing vast and real, but hazardous, market opportunities reachable through the use of appropriate technology. Hazardous because this customer may not be representative of a large number of customers with similar needs and yet his demand is influential. Should the hotel invest in an electronic mail system so that it can retain this customer? Was the wake-up call service appreciated? An automatic switch to turn on the TV may be quite adequate. Should video contacts replace the need to travel and, hence, displace the need for business hotels altogether? How should a TV manufacturer customize the sets for hotels and thereby secure that particular market niche? What should computer makers and software writers do to cash in on the wake-up call market or perhaps to ensure that they can gain a foothold in the electronic mail service market?

Our starting point is, therefore, a small but typical case of opportunities brought about by our real needs and our ability to meet them through the use of technology. No wonder decision-making is becoming infinitely complex for all users, service providers and manufacturers alike. How can a new product be envisaged and what does it take to introduce it successfully in the marketplace?

What infrastructure is needed to support this new product and how can the users be encouraged to take full advantage of it? The answers to these questions imply the necessary conditions for successful exploitation of any new business opportunity.

The solutions to these questions are, in general, totally elusive, but for specific cases, they can have unlimited opportunities. This situation transforms the very basis of established business practices and calls for new management techniques in all aspects of operations, engineering, marketing and sales. It is no wonder that success in personal computers and electronic gadgets for offices has been so sporadic and unpredictable. We shall begin by looking at what changes technology has wrought and why we have a confluence of achievements which should encourage the emergence of a whole host of good business opportunities.

Perhaps the most significant factor that technology has brought to us is the means for products to be tailored to meet and satisfy individual needs at affordable prices. This is a bold and sweeping statement which must be carefully explained and substantiated.

"Excellent choice," said the car salesman. "We'll have your car in metallic blue color, with factory-fitted stereo radio/cassette, an extra headrest, light alloy wheels and a 1.8 liter engine with turbo-charger readied very quickly. The turn-around time from our fully automated production lines is really good. Sorry that none of the cars here in stock meets your needs, but you'll only need to wait for two weeks. You may like to use our demonstration car in the meantime." The sale was amicably concluded. The customer turned to the salesman as they approached the door. "That is good, in two weeks I can have the car of my choice. Please tell me, how is the car factory organized to meet individual demands like mine when mass-production is needed to minimize cost?" "Well, sir, it baffles me, too. However, I could arrange for you to tour the factory. I went there once and was fascinated by the whole process of flexible mass-production."

"Ladies and gentlemen, a big welcome to our company. In the next hour you'll be conducted around this fully automated factory which produces a single basic car model with customized specifications." The tour guide of this car factory proudly welcomes his daily visitors. It is a routine job for him, but each time he faces a new crowd, anxious to hear about and see the mystery of car making, he anticipates a variety of expected and, yes, unexpected questions. He finds this a challenge. Besides, he knows that the tour is an important marketing action and the company's success is influenced by it. He is well satisfied with his job and warms up to the occasion.

"We will walk alongside the entire production line on a path-way which is routinely used for visitors but is also used as an inspection route. Every day a robot inspector makes periodic inspection tours. We aim for zero defects in our quality control and the robot inspector is a part of this process. At each major stage of production, I'll give some explanations and answer any questions you may have. Please follow me.

"We start our tour in this central control room. Here we have a visual display of the production status of our assembly lines. Here we load our production plan for the day, which specifies exactly the number of cars to be produced and the parts to be used for each. It is the brain of our factory and it initiates all actions." "A question, please," says one customer, "Who prepares the production plan and how can errors be detected or corrected?" "Well, sir, this is a very good question. Our production plan is not entirely error-proof. What we do is to make sure that machine errors are reduced to a very low limit. We aim at one in a trillion which is readily achievable in our electronic data processing equipment. We then reduce our human errors to a minimum by using the direct input from the dealer who prepared this data together with the customer. Perhaps you'll recall, if you have already ordered a car from us, that the dealer read back to you your requirements after he prepared your order. In this process he actually prepared your requirements on a computer input card and then obtained a printout of this which he checked with you. This way, there is no accumulation of human errors.

"Each day, the production plan is a string of car orders which specify with which parts and finishes each car is to be fitted. The input data is distributed electronically to the areas where the appropriate parts are loaded onto the conveyor belts. Then the belts are programmed to deliver the right parts to the right car at the right time. Human labor is involved only in the stocking of parts and in the assembly in this nearby assembly line. Even in the assembly area robots are used to relieve the monotonous assembly tasks. In fact, most human efforts are devoted to trouble shooting."

"What happens if a failure occurs at one section of the assembly line? Does it mean that the whole line has to stop? I would guess that the cost of idling time must be prohibitive," says a knowledgeable customer who is familiar with the process of manufacturing.

"Of course you are right; we cannot afford to have one or even several local problems along the assembly line that would shut down the entire factory. Generally speaking, we can accumulate sub-assemblies, so that the problems can be corrected while sub-assemblies continue to be produced. There is a trade-off between space requirements, capital investment and particularly the means to accelerate any process which has been out of action for a while. The solution is complex. In fact, it is the area where the production-control boys are working hardest. They try to minimize downtime of the equipment by preventive maintenance and to optimize the production-line rate applicable to different circumstances after a failure. I just heard that they have tried a new linear programming method which is supposed to be more efficient than the simplex. method. If this is successful, I predict that we can reduce the car price by at least 10%. That will give our competitors something to think about.

"As we go through this door, we'll be at the start of the assembly line. Please follow me. The first impression you'll have is the spaciousness of the line with hardly any people in it. Many lines of activities are simultaneously started here at the beginning. On the right are the chassis and rear wheel assembly. On the left is the engine with front wheel and transmission attachments. The people you see here are mainly inspectors. The parts assembly operations here are all automated.

"Here we see a critical stage where the engine is mounted on the chassis. Failure at this point will cause a considerable pile-up of engine assemblies and chassis assemblies. Therefore, several lines are in parallel here. Look to your left; you'll see the body-conveyor line. The finished bodies have gone through rust proofing, painting and baking before they reach the next assembly point where they will be mated to the engine/chassis assembly. The number of parallel lines is decreasing. Please note the different velocities of the various conveyor lines.

"All this time, the instructions of your specific order are being obeyed. This green car has a sunroof and an air-conditioner. It has a 5-speed manual shift, etc. Note that the process is really simple when everything is modularized. Well, it is simple after a hell-of-a-lot of work has gone into making the optional parts interchangeable. We have come a long way to make customer-specific cars. Without the computer we could never achieve this. Just look at all those localized computers in the robots, the big computers doing the control and programming of the parts and the other computers used by the designers to make parts compatible and interchangeable. We are really very lucky to be able to satisfy our customers' individual needs in a car so admirably."

"Hold on. I object to that," a somewhat irritated would-be customer retorts. "I wanted a two-tone body and you discontinued it last year. What about the anti-skid brake option; why can't you make that cheaper so that I can afford it? Why on earth do you not spend money on making this great safety feature affordable instead of spending money on research to provide drivers with automatic location indicators and street-map facilities when most of us know exactly where we are going most of the time?"

This story about cars contains many salient points. It illustrates the interrelationship between the customers' requirements which are part generic and part specific; the manufacturer's constraints on cost and product options; the salesman's position on selling and education as the linkage between customer and manufacturer; and technology's role in enabling the whole process of supply and demand to be met. It also indicates strongly that even with a well-established product, namely a car, the needs of the customer far exceed the basic function of the car. Technology enables the cost of production to be lowered while options increase. The car market becomes a mass market with built-in individualism. It is a mass-customed market. Opportunities for innovation are substantial. However, the cost reduction or increase with less or more features really makes marketing more complex and customer targeting more speculative. An increase in choice is always accompanied by more difficulties in decision-making, both for the manufacturer as well as the customer; this increases the importance of marketing.

Another example from the pharmaceutical industry illustrates further the consequences of technology-induced product proliferation.

In a board meeting at a leading pharmaceutical company the newly appointed chairman and CEO made his first recommendation.

"Gentlemen and ladies of the Board, I have carefully studied our research capabilities and assessed the complex new drug market. I have come to the conclusion that the cost of marketing a new drug is too large. We must take a longer-term view. I recommend to the Board that we channel our research resources towards the causes of disease instead of our current efforts of studying the effect of variants of drugs on a disease based on our current understanding. This is a highly innovative recommendation and is not made lightly."

The boardroom buzzed with excitement and some air of disbelief. The wily new CEO continued:

"When 300 or more types of Cortisone drugs are available for minor skin ailments, what can make a real impact in the marketplace? Doctors are flooded with advance notices of these brand-name products. They really cannot be bothered with another new addition, even if it has been shown to have several percent higher effectiveness. Patients are at an even greater loss since every advertisement extols the superior virtues of a product. If our research staff start by uncovering the basic causes of diseases and then explaining the nature of treatment, they are not only contributing greatly to knowledge but also are laying down very significant marketing strategies and directions. Naturally, we will be first to announce the new drugs, and our voice will be heard as the voice of authority instead of as an also-ran or, worse, as an outsider. I submit that there is no more sensible plan than this one. Besides, the research into the causes of diseases does not have to result in breakthroughs. A better and more logical presentation of the interpretation of our current understanding could enhance and guide our marketing efforts and increase the success of our research and development efforts on the more conventional drugs already under investigation. Furthermore, the research cost can in fact be recovered by lowering our wasteful marketing efforts in low-margin, crowded markets."

A respectful hush ensued. "I'd like to see a return-on-investment analysis done on this," said one Board member steeped in traditional thinking. "I do have an analysis ready for presentation here. However,

I debated as to the validity of it and decided not to table it. However, since you ask, I'll show it briefly. You'll see that the intermingling of R&D cost and marketing expenses makes the analysis less than convincing," said the CEO. "The comptroller felt, when we discussed this, that the return on investment can only be alluded to by assuming that several new drugs will be introduced per year as the result of this effort. The budget assumes an increase in the current research expenditure level and a reduction in the marketing expenses to reflect the marketing impact of research. The return on R&D is expected to increase with time and hopefully become very significant in a five to seven year time frame."

This shrewd move on the part of the CEO illustrates his appreciation that technology must be applied strategically before it can help the business significantly. Otherwise, the expense of developing the technology can easily be wasted. Furthermore, inappropriate application of technology to products could bring disastrous consequences. It adds development cost to products and results only in added features of marginal value. Even if the manufacturing and parts costs of the product are lowered, the development cost and increased marketing cost could lower profit margins markedly. On the other hand, technology allows products to be tailored better and to suit more exactly the real needs of customers. Identification of these opportunities where a company has the aspiration and sufficient skill in matching technology, marketing and management leads to new and improved products and to business successes. Implicit in this discussion is the assumption that technology is the *raison-d'être* of our increased opportunity. Technology can improve the quality of products, lower the cost, provide better functional design and, above all, intensify competition.

Which are the most influential developments in science and technology in recent years? Each member of a panel of ten experts could provide a convincing list of ten items, each related to the particular discipline of his expertise. With larger numbers of experts, longer lists should emerge. Perhaps the best way to seek meaningful answers to this question is to ask people in different walks of life for their opinions.

Politician: "I can reach the people. The newspapers, magazines, radio, telephone and particularly the TV allow me to let my views be heard, and to show people what I stand for. The media surely are powerful channels of communication. I vote for video technology as the most influential."

Medical Doctor: "My ability to do my job better derives from our capability to prevent, diagnose and cure diseases more effectively through a continuing improvement in the understanding of the causes of disease, particularly at the microscopic molecular level. Certainly, advanced diagnostic techniques such as X-ray, sonar and MRI tomography are powerful diagnostic aids which remove much of the risk involved in using surgical diagnostic methods."

Sociologist: "Computers help me a lot. They allow complex models of sociological evolutions to be tested. However, my problem is actually much more difficult, since with population increase un-abated, and rapid worldwide communication possible, social dis-content can be more acute, especially under an uneven social development. Besides, we now have three new phenomena: One is the enormous size of the aging population beyond retirement age. Medical advances are creating a large number of elderly people, many of whom are in poor health. Another phenomenon is the attitude of the young, who have the opportunity to gain more experience in a shorter time; this is causing them to become apa-thetic about self-advancement. The third is the reduction of human labor-intensive activities through the existence of efficient tools designed to remove the chores and improve productivity. This creates unemployment and aggravates social discontent. Social develop-ment is impacted very much by science and technology taken as a whole."

Economist: "I welcome the computers, the improved communi-cations and all the material and equipment now available to serve us. We are almost reaching the point where, when any economically significant action takes place, its effect can be felt almost instantly throughout the whole economic world. This makes the economic model real and the economic processes predictable. Computer technology is by far the most influential of technologies which alter the economy of the world. Who would have dreamed that thousands of people are now earning their keep by transferring money from one currency to another through electronic fund shifting?"

Mathematician: "I am not convinced that science and technology help mathematics very much. Sure, numerical techniques became an important branch of mathematics and have been developed extensively. However, abstract mathematical thinking transcends science and technology. I must admit that mathematics dealing with reasoning and intelligence does not exist, but mathematicians are currently being stimulated into action to create relevant mathematics by the scientific and technological advancement towards automata."

Scientist: "Quantum mechanics and relativity concepts allow atoms to be manipulated and electrons and photons to be harnessed. This advancement in microscopic material science has created new materials, helped to generate energy, and broadened our understanding in physics and chemistry."

Technologist: "Our scientific knowledge has been utilized to create building materials with desirable properties and electronic materials for making efficient devices which can work at higher speeds. It has opened up almost the entire electromagnetic energy spectrum for our exploitation and has created new measurement tools and apparatus for control and instrumentation."

In fact, crucial and important advances have been made on a wide front. As a result, we have three distinctly new situations:

1. Transportation systems for physical goods and messages that are highly transparent to capacity and distance. In particular, it will soon be possible to transfer messages in speech, data, graphics and video format instantly throughout the world to

provide an interactive facility that will change the role of the physical transport system for people and goods.

2. A signal processing system which allows data storage and manipulation, which can handle very large quantities of data, and can start to do rapid and intelligent processing. This permits the further extension of machine roles into our human efforts.

3. Materials can be synthesized from atoms and molecules which differ significantly from naturally formed raw materials. Molecular engineering is providing new materials in the forms of biomolecules, electronic materials and structural materials with special desirable properties.

The combination of these three areas of advancement at the same time is powerful. Our dream of Utopia takes on a different hue. Everything we want to do towards making ourselves more efficient and powerful appears to be possible. We can remove the constraints set by natural material properties and break the bottleneck of information indigestion, and we can deliver and communicate with practically no delays. This combination is so powerful that opportunities literally become unlimited. However, this is not without caveats. The available resources and time provide a delicate balance between good and poor opportunities. The risks and rewards of business remain the same even if opportunities abound. While in the former days product differentiation was highly important because opportunities were created more or less by variations on a few standard themes, the new situation now requires matching new products to real but not necessarily highly conscious needs. In other words, more effort is needed to create the market for the product.

A product strategy meeting is in progress. "At our last meeting we evaluated the strength of our company and decided to introduce a new product in order to increase our sales volume by an additional $100 million over a period of four years beginning two years from now," the secretary reminded everyone. Then he continued, "We are a traditional telecommunication equipment company with a few large, stable customers buying about 80% of our products. The other 20% are sold through a nationwide distribution network. We have strong RD&E activities and, particularly, we have recently invested heavily in our longer-term research efforts towards acquiring a good understanding of recent scientific and technological advancement and demonstrating a few attractive applications. Our traditional business can maintain its competitiveness through careful cost reduction and marginal performance improvement over the next five years and grow on average approximately 10% per annum. This will necessitate the expenditure of 5% of sales on RD&E, leaving 1% for new product development. Our current sales are in round figures $100 million. Therefore, we have about $1m/year for this new project over the next six years. The sales/R&D investment then will be 100/6 = 16 which is workable. The ROI target is to be 6% after taxes.

"A task force of six people has been established. It consists of marketing and engineering personnel, with our general manager participating on a part-time basis. Today we are here to listen and debate their recommendations. Ted is the task-force leader and he is going to kick-off this meeting."

Ted is an engineer with broad experience. His talent is particularly evident in his attention to details while maintaining a broad viewpoint, yet at the same time being able to keep to the point. He begins: "Our job turned out to be relatively simple after we adopted an effective two-prong approach. We started by listing some desirable opportunities and then looked at the resources needed, both technology and marketing-wise. We quickly arrived at a much reduced and particularized list of possible products representing new opportunities. Then we weighed the risks and rewards by matching the opportunity to resource requirements and put in the time factor. At that point, only a few products remained viable as opportunities. We assessed how these could meet our ROI objectives. Of course, our conclusions are non-exclusive, but they met our company's growth requirements.

"I'd like to thank my colleagues on this task force for their cooperative spirit. I must say we did this very efficiently. Apart from three days of concentrated work, we did much of the preparatory work over the last three months along with our normal day-to-day duties and only had ten other short meetings to keep in touch.

"In this first chart I have listed the desirable attributes of any new product:

1. Plays a role between switching and transmission products.
2. Can be used individually or as part of a complete system.
3. Meets real needs.
4. Does not require an excessive amount of yet-to-be-developed technology.
5. The users are mainly within our customer base.

"These turn out to be a summary of factors which have a great deal of impact on resource requirements and time factors. They also have implications for providing a future base for expansion.

"Let me comment briefly on each of these five attributes:

"1. Plays a role between switching and transmission products.

"We are traditionally a company making switching and transmission products. It is a huge advantage to expand in an area away from, but related to, the main stream. This reduces resource requirements and poses little threat to our existing business. Hence, we choose a new product with a role between switching and transmission.

"2. Can be used individually or as part of a complete system.

"The cost and timing to develop a product having several parts which together form a complete system may be longer than for single products, but this requirement generates product synergy. At the same time it encourages the architecture of the product to be designed with modularity and flexibility. It is a necessary design criterion.

"3. Meets real needs.

"The criterion to meet real needs is, as it were, a commandment in marketing. This criterion can be met more readily by the greatly improved availability of technology.

"For example, the 4 kHz voice from the telephone is adequate for our needs, since we can recognize and feel the familiarity of the voice even if it is somewhat distorted. However, graphic images transmitted over telephone lines using old facsimile equipment are poor in quality reproduction and are inadequate for our needs. It served an important role in the input since it was the only means we had for fast graphic document transmission. A high-quality graphic-image transmission system will meet the desired transmission image standard and will eliminate the need for the old system.

"4. Does not require an excessive amount of yet-to-be-developed technology.

"The temptation to use yet-to-be-developed technology to enhance product differentiation is high. It is important to bear in mind that a trade-off between performance and timing and cost is involved when yet-to-be-developed technology must be used.

"5. The users are mainly within our customer base.

"Obviously this arrangement would give us synergy in our marketing efforts. It can reduce our marketing costs for the new products.

"After weighing the options our recommendations are:

- a private electronic exchange PBX for multiple services,
- a personal workstation,
- a high-resolution high-speed FAX system.

"Each of these meets the sales volume and investment requirements, while all should meet the ROI objectives and timing."

The meeting went on with presentations of technologies involved, skill mixes, and competitive issues. The issues which dominated most of the discussion were: "Can we draw up a specification for this product? How should we evolve the performance over the lifetime of this product? What should be the life of the product?" It can be argued that this situation is true for all products conceived by all competitors. It became clear that by limiting the target objectives the risks can be minimized, while the return on investment is still reasonable. It was also clear that the risk analysis is easier if technology trends can be firmly predicted.

As the discussion continued, a person from the marketing department remarked, "Voice-activated dialing for PBX is a feature desired by a lot of people. Why do you recommend that it should not be offered? In my opinion voice-activated dialing can make this product more appealing to special groups."

"I believe that you have stated your question correctly; indeed, we recommend no voice dialing because we feel that the customer base for such a product is different from the one we are targeting. We are targeting a PBX which serves to interconnect multifunction equipment to the telephone lines with a great deal of flexibility and at a cost attractive to a relatively large customer base. Our PBX product can accept equipment with voice-activation features, but this is different from providing such a feature. For one thing, voice-activated dialing introduces a new technology requirement which involves relatively high risks. Betty, would you be kind enough to clarify this point for our marketing friend?"

Betty is an electronic integrated-circuit expert with a broad experience base. Betty starts emphatically: "Product obsolescence is higher if we need custom LSI circuits, since these custom LSI circuits are designed to offer specific features. For complex circuits produced in relatively small volumes the cost is high. The voice-recognition chip is particularly vulnerable. Voice-recognition technology is at a relatively early stage of development, such that even for the limited vocabulary set needed for voice-activated dialing, the circuit complexity is high. Furthermore, someone could develop a much more efficient voice-recognition scheme in the near future which could change the circuit cost by an order of magnitude. We made an analysis of the investment return and rejected it as requiring too many resources for the benefit generated."

"Are you saying that we should be content to let the competitors make our new product obsolete?"

"Not at all. Remember, we must always have a specific target market for each product. We can choose the option of offering voice dialing if it is our marketing goal. Betty is just pointing out a technology risk which led the task force not to recommend our new product for the customers who will buy equipment with voice-dialing features. In fact, we are not exactly opting out. Our equipment will be a new PBX, specially designed to provide maximum interconnection efficiency at a very attractive cost. Furthermore, it wholly interconnects equipment that has voice-dialing features."

Betty added, "If the question is whether a chip set to provide voice-dialing can be designed to meet a certain cost target, the answer is of course, 'Yes.' It makes sense if your business aim is to market such a chip set to equipment makers who want to provide voice-dialing features. This chip set will have a relatively short market life, but if the ROI target can be met, it is a viable business, even if it is to be produced in one production run only. What I was commenting on earlier really referred to the equipment maker making the additional investment to custom design such a chip set. I must hasten to add that for certain other companies this could make sense. They may have a range of products all of which could benefit from simple voice-recognition features. The investment, then, for a special chip set could be conceivable. Please note that simple voice-recognition features and voice-dialing features are likely to be similar. Nevertheless, if the recognition is to be in English spoken by a non-native speaker, the time scale for such a technology development can be much longer. A feature of our recommended product is not to exclude voice dialing but to make sure that no competitor can outsell us by offering all our features.

"This brings up the point about opportunities unlimited. The ins and outs of a product in terms of its features and functions are highly complex. What we do is to reduce the opportunities by matching a target customer base for which real needs exist to a tailored product. What is awaiting us are the essentials for creating the market for our product in the target customer base by marketing actions. Our marketing friend Joe in our task force will say a few words on this."

Joe is a traditional marketing man with a firm belief that traditional methods are important. However, he is convinced of the concept
that a new market does not exist by itself. It must be created. What
convinced him is the fact that he was not able to spell out his real
needs for which he subconsciously had a feel. He found that if he
does spell out a specific real need, he may find several ways of
satisfying it equally well, or he may find that he must accept a
compromise. He longs for a better life and an easier decision making-
process. In his guts, he knows that is what marketing is all about.
Recently he felt magnanimous. He devoted a lot of his energy towards
satisfying his longing which he regarded as a common "want" of a
good many people. He is doing lots of good as he puts it. Indeed,
what Joe has been doing is to highlight the problem underlying the
identification of need as a new marketing tool.

Joe approached the dais and smiled broadly. "I know what you
want. You want a product which wholly decide for us what our new
products should be. Well, I am what you want." The audience
laughed politely. "As our task force delved into this, I was more
convinced than ever that we have, even after we narrowed it down
to three product types, a large variety of choices. I am equally convinced that the final choice of one or more specific products in these
product types makes little difference in our ability to be successful,
and anyone is almost equally good. The difference is in the marketing steps. These must have a common structure but a great deal of
detailed implementation differences.

"It is equally good because our customers-to-be really need it.
However, they are not making their demands in unison. They are not
in a position to, since variations of their requirements as individuals,
or from company to company, do exist. Just as for automobiles, the
need is well appreciated but variations within it are many. It is equally
good for us, since we have more or less optimized our resources and
advantages.

"From the marketing point of view, what I must do is to assess
who are the customers-to-be who could be effectively coaxed into

believing that their needs can be fulfilled and that this particular need is high on their list of priorities, and finally, that they can easily afford it. In fact, they cannot afford to be without it, since the benefit, if not taken, will appear as a deficiency in their own endeavors. Of course, these are traditional precepts for good marketing. The reasons for trade have not changed. Nevertheless, the difference in our new environment is the abundance of choice. I must help my customers to help themselves by buying my product. In other words, they must be fully convinced that I have identified their needs and have got what it takes to meet these needs. My marketing must start with an awareness campaign of the virtues of this product which our company is developing to meet their need. This should start immediately after our decision to make this product. Our targeted customers will receive information and a timetable to help them with their planning process. There will be communication channels set up to encourage interaction. If all goes according to plan, then in one-to-two years' time, when our product is ready for delivery, orders equal to our market projection should result. The secret is to target well and to do everything within the resource budget and make it happen as nearly as possible as planned. Hand-waving estimates are never sufficient. Even well-conceived statistical methods of selling are no longer effective since new markets must literally be created from zero. I must repeat: This is forced upon us, because making choices from an abundance of options is too difficult for everyone.

"Obviously, this is really a leadership strategy. It is foolhardy to assume that competitors are not doing exactly the same, or that they are riding on the coat-tail of our effort and preparing to beat us to the bell by introducing the exact product before we are ready. Therefore, once the decision is made, an all-out effort is needed. Since we have optimized our resources and advantages, we should have a better or at least an equal chance of reaching the tape first. Of course, if our advantages are marginal, then we have to aim for a smaller percentage share. On the other hand, our competitors cannot come in cold. If my marketing is effective, they will have to do a lot of fast talking to convince our customers that they too can be trusted.

"That, you see, is the importance of doing complete marketing. It is a case of recognizing the key aspects and launching the best plan of attack. Again I am lapsing into trusted rules of marketing."

"What about product differentiation? You have said nothing about it so far, and several years ago I heard you stressing product differentiation repeatedly," an engineer in the audience shouted out.

"Oh yes. Product differentiation! I tried to understand its role within the new environment which technological changes have brought. As a marketing person, I like to say that my product is better because it has this feature or that function which my competitors' products do not offer. However, the rules of our game have changed. We have no homogeneous market where we are trying to carve our niche. We are creating. Remember that. We are creating new markets to replace the old homogeneous market. So product differentiation is not needed. You have the unique product for the unique market which you have just created, to satisfy a unique set of real needs. If a competitor comes along with a product with additional features and at the same price and delivery, your market share will be seriously eroded. However, the optimization, made before the product introduction decision, takes out much of this risk. In a real situation, the competitors may get a fraction of your targeted customer base. If we are lucky, we could also erode somebody else's customer base a little. We are dealing with cultivated real needs."

"I am still not convinced that we can cultivate real needs. There are so many significant parameters which affect the marketing effort. How do you try to bound the risk, given rather finite resources?" the engineer insisted.

"This is a serious issue. This is why ambitious new businesses are so difficult. If we knew the answer, we'd all be millionaires. High risk and large reward often go hand in hand. In a company like ours, we are prepared to take certain risks and we just have to set our reward sight accordingly. As our information age progresses, those with better ways of gathering and understanding information and disseminating it could have a competitive edge and thereby get a larger share of the profit. This also means that those who can understand customers' needs better in the information age can also reap a higher share of the profits. My contention today is to emphasize that our new product must have a new market which is explicitly designed and erected for it. This closure of events, i.e. completeness of planning, is a necessary criterion for success."

"Can you comment on the voice-dialing feature in the context of what you have just said?" "Sure. I am with Betty. She is as much a part of marketing in her role as a part of engineering. She is helping marketing when the marketing requirements are translated into minimum cost and maximum flexibility. The focus of the product as a multifunctional equipment interconnection device is different from a voice-dialing feature. Her authoritative voice will guide our customers' recognition of their choice of options.

"Efficient planning and resource utilization with precise targeting are of paramount importance when new business opportunities are to be selected to augment or replace current business. The opportunities are unlimited, but for each established company only few options are really worth exploiting and only a few can be exploited with available resources."

This theme has been emphasized throughout this chapter. Indeed, throughout this book evidence to support this will be mounting.

Taking this situation as a whole, the true benefactors are ourselves. A confluence of technology has opened up unlimited business opportunities, many of which will improve not marginally but significantly our quality of life. For each individual and each enterprise, the consequence of abundance is highly positive provided we avoid indigestion and target our endeavor on a narrow and affordable path. As we progress further in our information age, we will manage information better and our opportunity path will broaden appreciably.

Chapter 2

A Changing Business Environment

Everyone has his own supply and demand requirements. In a time of abundance, Peter has a well-paid job. He is able to buy most of what he wants, and lives rather comfortably. In a time of scarcity, Paul has a poorly paid job or no job and must try his hardest to make ends meet. He lives a mere existence. However, even Peter could feel miserable because he could not afford a Porsche instead of his Buick, while Paul might be exhilarated because he was able to buy two oranges at a nickel apiece. The vicissitudes of life make abundance and scarcity highly relative and complicated. Nevertheless, supply and demand, the basis of business, are closely linked with abundance and scarcity.

In the pre-industrial age, traders had a low rank in the social strata. Above them were the workers, the farmers and the scholars—in that order. The lord of the manor ruled over his little community within a feudalistic state. His farmers produced the food, his workers attended to craft and construction tasks. The scholars had the knowledge and were capable of rising to influential positions either on their own or by supporting a leader. The traders merely moved along the sidelines, attempting to provide a service or to promote the conclusion of a barter.

Time moved along and was not noticed by the people. Time was not very meaningful; it was merely a period in which one grew from infancy to old age. "Dust thou art and unto dust shalt thou return." There were many unknowns, but that was the mystery of life. There was no time to contemplate, only time to carry out the routine tasks of hard labor. That was part of life—one's lot—as one would say. Joy and pathos, life and death, work and play, everything was linked with the immediacy of living. The human desires were well bounded and technology—"Never heard of it!"—was not even a word in the dictionary.

Even then life was not peaceful. Wars were long and bitter. They were fought on many pretexts: religion, idealism and others. Essentially, war was a quick means to acquire what others had and add it to the winner's coffer and, thereby, increase the sense of his security through having an abundance of goods.

As life experiences increased, it became generally recognized that productivity and trade could make life better for everyone. Adam Smith proposed the theory of capitalism, which he hailed as the salvation of the people. At the same time, science had reached a point where applications were possible. The great Industrial Revolution was poised to begin.

Of course, this is not a book on history and the events enumerated are conveniently arranged to bring out the essence of society in the pre-industrial revolution days and to illustrate how the economy revolved around a small, more or less self-contained community.

Evidently, in this period trade did not play an influential role in shaping history or extending our civilization. Merchants did not control in any way the abundance or scarcity of commodities satisfying the needs and wants of the majority. It is not surprising that their lot was to be at the bottom of the totem pole.

As the Feudal Ages gradually gave way to Republics, trade made steady progress. More people were engaged in producing wares for the consumption of many. The transport systems on land and sea permitted goods to be moved from almost anywhere in the world. The demand for the rare and exotic enriched the adventuresome as well as those who organized and distributed these precious commodities. Trade emerged as a necessary aspect of life and the status of merchants rose in the social hierarchy.

When the Industrial Age dawned, manufacturers assumed great power. The voracious demand of the people increased the power of the producers of goods. Raw materials, finished consumer items, food and construction materials were all needed in greater quantities than the rate of production. The industrialists exploited this for personal gain and for the well-being of a minor portion of the community at the expense of the masses. Wages were minimal, working conditions were poor and manual labor was the order of the day. Of course, there were counter-balancing forces. There were philanthropic industrialists, scholars and rulers whose humanitarian spirit rose above sheer greed and gluttony. They abhorred the animal-like treatment meted out in certain types of work and were horrified by the prevalence of child labor.

The flaunting of justice and fairness was intolerable to the upright people who fought for liberty, equality and the pursuit of happiness. Slowly, and gradually, this condition of gross inequality was reduced. Adam Smith and Karl Marx represented the extreme ends of idealistic views. The former saw the good of a free market, the latter saw the need for total sharing of the fruits of labor. The economics of trade and industry had now emerged as a dominant factor in our life.

At that stage, the different levels of economic development of the various parts of the world were only loosely influencing each other. China, the Central Kingdom, was large, prosperous and self-contained. She did not need to have any contacts outside what she defined as her domain. Europe was the center of the Industrial Revolution and, for a while, it was content with the far-from-saturated markets in its own land. The United States was a land which had just been discovered, a mere 300 plus years prior, by Columbus and a small number of other adventurers.

Within each country the development was localized. The local needs tended to be met by local enterprises. In England, Newcastle was a center for coal production. This led to such common sayings as "bringing coals to Newcastle" as a statement of ridicule. It was a situation of having well-known, easily identifiable needs awaiting to be satisfied by products and services designed and produced to meet these needs. "By the sweat of thy brow shall you be rewarded," claimed the epitome of work ethics. No wonder, in those days there was no need to have business schools. Opportunities abounded and were easily identified. All one needed was the will to apply oneself and make it happen. It was no surprise to see capitalism working like magic. With free markets and a free-enterprise system, an individual could make a fortune through hard work. In one venture, he would have created many jobs and paid out a lot of wages which the people working for him could spend. He had increased the wealth of the total population and benefited mankind and himself. He was the spirit, motivator, organizer and philanthropist, as well as the deserving recipient.

Not content with the prospect that the needs of the people could be gradually satisfied at a manual rate of production, industrialists pushed for mechanization and manufacturing techniques to improve productivity per capita. Aided by man's ingenuity, the great technology development started. Levers increased our muscular strength, wheels made things move easily, gears were levers to rotation. Steam engines provided mechanical horsepower. Then came electricity, a form of energy which could be generated in large quantities and easily distributed and which could be used to drive motors producing power just as the steam engines did. The adaptation of technology to assist manual labor met with great success. By the end of the nineteenth century and the beginning of the twentieth century, technology started to impact business and continued with increasing influence into our present day and will continue into the foreseeable future.

Many items could be produced with the aid of machines at ten, or a hundred, or even thousands of times faster. Suddenly the conduct of business had to be revised. The local market could easily be saturated and new markets, in more distant lands, had to be reached. This required more action by the distribution side of the business. Agents were needed to scout out good new areas and to handle transportation. Shops were needed to distribute the goods. Communications between the agents, better means of transportation, etc. had to be developed. Soon Europe started to look beyond itself as part of its market zone. In return, the raw materials consumption rose to such an extent that importation from distant lands had to be considered.

In the manufacturing area, the faster product flow gave rise to many new organizational requirements. Maintenance, quality control, material flow, work flow, and inventory control were some of the new tasks with interrelated impacts. The management structure, worker deployment and working procedures had to be reorganized. Hundreds of details had to be seen to. The aim was to apply technology and management to increase and maximize productivity per capita. At the same time the business entities had long since grown to sizes beyond the ability of a single person to supervise and control. Many businesses also had been set up as corporations to enable more capital to be raised through the combination of resources of several individual enterprises or, more broadly, from a variety of large and small investors. This move generated the new scenario that corporations were to be managed by a group of people who must work to achieve the expectations of the investors.

The story of General Electric Company (GE) at that time, when organization and methods (OM) were the latest rage of good practice at factories, is instructive to recount. GE had an assembly plant for lamp bulbs. The OM department carried out an experiment with a view to increase the productivity of the workers for that task. The experiment was to determine whether ambient light in the assembly area affected the productivity. They divided the work area into two sections and informed the operators about the experiment, that the light level would be adjusted in one area only and their output would be compared with that in the other. They found that each time the light level was increased, productivity increased. Then to their complete surprise, each time the light level was lowered, productivity also increased, even at the point when the workers were working practically without seeing. What the OM people ignored was the human spirit. The results came from the workers' perceptions that changes in the levels of light were a challenge to them. The ease of assembly caused by better lighting was not responsible for the results of this experiment.

OM is representative of many branches of pseudo-science and psychology developed during the heydays when technology altered the methods of production. The intentions of OM were clear, but as a universal cure for management problems and as a means of increasing productivity per capita, it fell far short of its goals. Nevertheless, this is a hindsight view. At that time OM represented an important step towards production improvement. Along with OM was the start of great analyses of business and management as a new discipline for advanced studies. Between 1955 and 1975 the views, visions, analyses, conclusions and recommendations on how to do business grew thick and fast.

According to a selection of key articles published in the *Harvard Business Review* over that period, the range of topics and prevalent views shows the broad basis of functional activities encompassed in the operations and conduct of businesses and some degree of changing concerns in each of these broad areas.

"General Management and Administration" contains the titles:

> Good Managers Do Not Make Policy Decisions
> Skills of an Effective Administrator
> Understanding Your Organization's Character
> Management by Whose Objectives?

Qualitative Insights from Quantitative Methods
Better Decisions with Preference Theory

"Planning and Strategy" shows a distinct awareness of the limitations and extent of usefulness of such activities. Examples are:

The President and Corporate Planning
Balance "Creativity" and "Practicality" in Formal Planning
Formulating Strategy in Smaller Companies

"Marketing" indicates some awareness that marketing involves laying the right foundation and not just sales. However, the market is always taken as existing and not as having to be created.

Marketing Myopia
Marketing Planning for Industrial Products
Get the Most Out of Your Sales Force
Manage the Customer, Not Just the Sales Force
Demarketing—Yes, Demarketing
Grass Roots Market Research

"Finance" is a formal discipline to be applied rigorously to meet the business needs.

Framework for Financial Decisions
How to Evaluate New Capital Investments
New Framework for Corporate Debt Policy

"The Individual and the Organization" points in a direction far beyond the original views of management and workers. The understanding of human motivation and limitations is emphasized.

Improving the Quality of Work Life
One More Time: How Do You Motivate Employees?
How to Deal with Resistance to Change
Executives as Human Beings
Interpersonal Barriers to Decision-Making

"Production and Operations" has grown from simple OM to the awareness of the need to attend to many different aspects of the business.

Manufacturing—Missing Link in Corporate Strategy
Production Planning and Control Integrated
Requirements Planning for Inventory Control
Sweeping Changes in Distribution
Production-Line Approach to Service
New Templates for Today's Organizations
Evolution and Revolution as Organizations Grow
How the Multidimensional Structure Works at Dow Corning
Strategy for Winning Employee Commitment
Can the Best Corporations Be Made Moral?

Also included in the *Harvard Business Review* is a key article demonstrating the growing awareness of the need for good information: "The Well-Read Manager," by J. B. Bennett and R. L. Weiher, made the need for adequate information abundantly clear.

Throughout this period, technology was making rapid advances in scope and complexity. Transistors and computers made their entry. At the same time, since the end of World War II, during which occurred the largest destruction of materials and goods in human history, the reconstruction boom has progressed unabated. By the early 1970s, the volume of business in the world had reached a very high level. Companies expanded. Corporations grew larger and larger. The race to put a man on the moon, the arms race and the great consumer-products race all promoted the use of technology in the service of men. It was "big is beautiful" since bigness increased total revenue. Flexibility in meeting cash-flow requirements and more synergy for resource utilization were the major goals.

While customers' demands were sky-rocketing and changing from essential goods to frivolities, the essence of business success was to make the process of producing goods or services satisfy the demands efficiently and effectively. The more streamlined the control of this logistic operation, the more prosperous the company could be. The bigger the corporation the larger the total profit, even if the operations were not as efficient. The resources needed to conduct business could be minimal since the markets were there waiting to be addressed. Companies grew, ranging from one-product specialists to conglomerates with practically no product commonality among their operating units. The *Fortune* 500 top companies in the world were dealing with a quarter of the world's commerce.

By the mid-1970s several basic changes had taken place. The customer community found that life was more than just material possessions. Furious consumption gave rise to natural-resource shortages and huge waste-disposal problems. At the same time, technology had made the world much smaller. Even the remotest corner of the world could be reached within hours. Furthermore, worldwide coverage by TV brought about an awareness of the standards of living in the different countries of the world and the quality of life of their peoples. The developing nations had grown to play an important role in the manufacturing of products, and the worldwide population with low per-capita income grew to enormous numbers.

This situation was very different from the previous one. The demands of the customers had changed. In the developed nations quality, reliability and purpose of products were required to satisfy the customers' perceptions of their needs. Moreover, most customers in advanced countries felt that they had reached an adequate level of satisfaction derived from the existing products. In the developing nations, the problem of how to meet the basic needs of a vastly increased population precluded any endeavors to promote trivial pursuits and frivolities. The desire for self-sufficiency also drove these nations to import the knowhow and to start their own production. Last, and certainly not least, technology has grown so much that a machine can replace many persons and achieve a higher output. This has caused a shortage of meaningful work for large numbers of people in the product-making areas. In many cases only machines can make certain products. A nation can be richer and more contented with a higher productivity per capita even if 20% of her workforce are unemployed. The important thing is to raise, on a worldwide basis, productivity per capita, which is an indicator of the quality of life of all human beings in the world.

Under this scenario, there are protectionism, increased competition, and an emphasis on small being also beautiful, etc. Few companies or corporations have responded, failing to recognize the changed environment. Some are still pressing on without change, but others are beginning to notice and to take actions more appropriate to the conduct of business under this new scenario.

It is difficult to ascertain the extent to which the nature of this impact is attributable to technology. Technology can be used to make practically everything and thereby presents us with an infinity of opportunities in a state of abundance. It is sufficient to repeat here that a major purpose of this book is to develop and clarify this statement.

Chapter 3

An Abundance of Scientific Knowledge

Early scientific developments appeared to be sporadic, non-systematic and intertwined with religion and social order. This was hardly surprising since communication was slow and poor, especially over long distances. Everything was wrapped in mystery and lacked satisfactory explanations. Our destiny seemed to be very much out of our control. In spite of this situation, the wonderment of nature touched our hearts. A small but select group of people took up the challenge to find some framework and order with which to explain natural phenomena. Astronomy was one of the oldest and most challenging of these frameworks. Geniuses like Aristotle laid very firm foundations to modern astronomy. Over 1,500 years later Copernicus and Kepler renewed the concept of a solar system with the sun as the center and the planets, including our earth, revolving around it. Galileo made astronomy an exact science, but had to face accusations of being a heretic.

On the more practical side, the inventions of stone tools and fire were stages in our struggle for basic survival. Herbal medicine and the art of healing developed on a highly practical ground. The early Iron Age also happened empirically. Even though alchemy had been practised for a long time, knowledge of chemistry was rudimentary.

Gradually knowledge accumulated. The sharing of experience became more common. After the invention of the printing press by Gutenburg in Europe and equivalent inventions elsewhere, the dissemination of knowledge became more widespread. The momentum of scientific development was gathering. In the Newtonian Age three pillars of knowledge emerged: the mathematicians, the physicists and the chemists. They succeeded in systematically putting a scientific base together, which allowed natural phenomena to have rational explanations. Each group, however, developed its own world even though, occasionally, their worlds overlapped somewhat.

Mathematicians revelled in logical reasoning, in constructing proofs and deductions, in logically consistent descriptions of numbers, geometrical shapes and their abstractions. Countable numbers were extended to rational, irrational and imaginary numbers. The study of number relationships became known as algebra. Physical shapes of lines, areas and solids were distilled into their properties in a study called geometry, and in turn were abstracted to non-physical objects of n-dimensions. Algebraic description was also used to describe geometry. The concepts of infinity and infinitesimal sizes led to the field known as calculus.

Physicists concentrated on physical phenomena. They studied the laws of motion and constructed the field of mechanics to link motion with force and distance. The properties of visible light became the field of optics. Sound waves, magnetism and electricity soon yielded their phenomenological secrets under the assault of the physicists. Apart from some odd phenomena which were neatly discarded, physicists in the Newtonian Age were convinced that they had the explanation for all natural phenomena.

Chemists attacked the secret of universal understanding from a different starting point. They argued that since everything was made up of some basic elements, if they could find all the elements, they would know how every matter came about. They succeeded marvellously. The periodic table, listing all the elements of which the world is made, was a triumph, not only because it was comprehensive, but also because it provided an easy way to categorize the properties of the elements. For example, at a glance one can identify an element as a gas or as a metal, determine its weight relative to others, its reactivity, its affinity to certain other elements, etc. Chemists also succeeded in predicting and controlling chemical reactions to produce new materials.

The three groups coexisted, and the progress of each was not greatly hindered by any lack of progress of the others. Occasionally, the physicists would like to have had better mathematical tools to help them, while chemists sometimes liked to try an explanation in physicists' terms.

This made the knowledge base relatively easy to maintain and develop. In school, mathematics, physics and chemistry were taught and then emphasized for students preparing for a career in one of those three specialist areas where universities offered separate degrees.

In the meantime, a technological revolution was in progress. The basic scientific knowledge was found to be valuable and was increasingly applied to solve technological problems. Engineers built houses and bridges with the aid of knowledge in mechanics; they developed radio and TV with the aid of knowledge in electricity and magnetism which, in the meantime, had evolved into the subject of electromagnetic fields and waves. Cars and aeroplanes were built with the combined knowledge of mechanics and material properties.

At the dawn of the Einstein Age, the neat compartmentalization of scientific subjects began to break down. Einstein's theory of relativity, which paved the way for establishing the subject of quantum mechanics, allowed the sub-atomic world to be brought to our attention. Physicists and chemists who had been studying the macroscopic world in physical and chemical terms found that the sub-atomic world offered a common basis for explaining both physical and chemical phenomena. Density, specific heat, dissociation energy, Le Chatelier's principle, the second law of thermodynamics, etc. are all revelations of the sub-atomic properties of matter.

Physicists busily developed sub-atomic physical theories such as the Solid State Theory, while chemists also proceeded along the same line and developed the Theory of Catalysis. Both resorted to sub-atomic mechanisms for more generalized explanations. All of a sudden, the background training and the tools to be used for these two branches of science began to converge rapidly.

Moreover, technologists had been successful in making science work for them. The successful invention of transistors, based on an understanding of the sub-atomic nature of materials, was opening up unprecedented opportunities to create a vast range of equipment to satisfy latent but truly significant needs. The computer, which could not be realized without the transistor, was one such example. Transistors in integrated circuit forms were soon to be found in almost all products that provided control and human-like capabilities. Future advances are expected to emerge through the combined application of a large number of interrelated fields of specialization.

The original situation of the Newtonian Age, with mathematics, physics and chemistry as the basic sciences, has undergone two significant changes. One is proliferation. The sub-branches of mathematics, physics and chemistry have grown to many. The second change is the rise of interrelationships. The overlap between physics and chemistry, in particular, has become prevalent. Both must resort more to the application of mathematics. These two changes make basic scientific training initially very complex, but this should eventually be easier.

As for the technologists, they face similar problems with similar degrees of difficulty. The fields of specialization extend well beyond civil, mechanical, chemical and electrical engineering. Materials, computers, information, automation and a host of other fields are emerging as important future engineering areas of specialization. At this stage, the depth of specialization and the breadth of background scientific knowledge are particularly challenging aspects for universities and other advanced educational institutions to ponder over in the training of engineers.

The temporary problem of having our scientific and technology base subdivided into a large number of specializations is, indeed, a serious one. The information generated from these areas are often related, sometimes significantly, but the rate of information generation is so great that we are literally flooded and drowning. We currently have no means to use the entire output effectively or to take advantage of their interrelationships. We cannot avoid duplication of effort or stop unproductive work through experience gained from another specialization field. Even results in the same field tend to be insufficiently and ineffectively communicated.

To complicate matters further, our technological development is at a stage where our hope to build a bridge to the linguistic and philosophical aspects of our knowledge from our scientific basis is rekindled. The computers and artificial intelligence work are holding forth a promise that we might be able to extend our brain functions. We have great hope of being able to tame the abundance of knowledge by condensation. We feel the urgency. We must perfect the tools to tame the consequence of our abundance of knowledge before we invest too much of our valuable, but limited, resources ineffectively. Indeed, these tools, if perfected, will also bridge the gap of knowledge and understanding. Alas, this is going to be a "bridge too far" for some time.

Let us take two examples, one to illustrate how extensively a knowledge base is involved with a relatively straightforward engineering task, the other to illustrate the commonality of the background knowledge needed to study physics and philosophy. These should demonstrate a little more clearly where we stand with respect to knowledge and understanding.

The engineering task is to make a "brick." The common brick used for house construction has been in use for thousands of years.

Initially they were simply made from clay from the ground, shaped when wet into a nearly rectangular shape, and dried in the air. These bricks, of course, will soften in continuous rain over an extended period. Then came the bricks which were heated to a high temperature in a fire. These bricks were found to be hard and water resistant, although moisture could seep through very slowly. A modern-day brick is still made from clay, but the composition of the clay is known and controlled. The particle size of the ingredients and the type of ingredients govern the color, texture and weight of the brick. The durability, hardness and water permeability are also dependent on the composition. Hence, a brick engineer needs certain knowledge about the composition of chemicals and their properties so as to appreciate the effect of variation in firing temperatures. He must know the thermal design of the furnace so that a load of bricks will experience temperatures within the tolerance permitted. He must also know the type of heating condition, whether the bricks will undergo oxidation or reduction due to the presence or absence of excess oxygen. He should have some idea of how to test brick for strength in tension, compression and shear. Also, he must be aware of how to get the constituent chemicals analyzed for acceptability. Since the exhaust from the kiln is toxic, he also needs to know toxic waste disposal procedures and/or toxic waste treatment.

If his company makes more than bricks for house building, he may be involved in heat-resistant bricks for kilns that have a composition requiring firing temperatures which are not easily reached without well-insulated large kilns. Bricks for the space shuttle are probably the most sophisticated bricks ever made. They are designed as a heat shield for the space shuttle during re-entry into the earth's atmosphere. The heat generated by friction with air must be insulated from the inner body of the space craft. The heat-shield bricks are designed as a heat insulator as well as a heat dissipator. Much research was needed to understand how to reduce heat conduction for material structures which must also retain mechanical strength. A porous body made with ultra-pure silica eventually emerged as a solution. The brick consisted of a mesh of silica fibers fused in such a way that a rigid structure formed with entrapped regions of void. High-purity ssilica fibers have a low expansion coefficient, a low thermal conductivity and a high melting point and will vaporize under extreme heat. These properties enabled the brick to act as an insulator and as a heat dissipator. The entire process of this development involved people trained in many disciplines ranging from material technologists to physicists to structural engineers.

Of particular interest is the fact that even a relatively simple product, when analyzed, shows that a host of scientific technical knowledge is needed for thorough understanding. Knowledge, furthermore, can enhance, improve, extend, alter, adapt and, above all, tailor the product for a target application. Throughout this book, and especially in the next three chapters, the reader will witness how knowledge sharpens our awareness of new possibilities and, in turn, provides us with the means to further our efforts towards creating a higher quality of life. In other words, our future needs are fulfilled through the application of our knowledge and skills.

In contrast, if we examine how the field of physics has progressed and compare it with how the field of philosophy has progressed, we immediately notice the difference between scientists and philosophers in the way in which they handle knowledge and understanding. Scientists create a framework to explain natural phenomena and to provide linkages between them and, in addition, to bring to our attention through extrapolation those realities which often escape our consciousness. The philosopher, on the other hand, seeks an explanation of his own senses and feelings. He tries to get a consistent interpretation, but he accepts human proneness to error and inconsistencies. Philosophers are able to tackle many problems from which scientists shy away. Socrates, Goethe, Confucius and Russell all advanced theories on human good and evil and the purpose of life. Scientists merely describe how matter is formed, how things work and have only recently attempted to touch upon the origin of life. The commonality of thoughts do occur though, particularly in the area of logic, which is regarded as the basis of rational thinking and reasoning.

"The pen is mightier than the sword," is an old English saying depicting the power of suggestion. This statement merely emphasizes that the decision process can be influenced more easily by direct appeal to our power of reasoning than through physical punitive power. It also suggests the closeness of our thinking process with our linguistic skill. Yet, at the same time words can carry different meanings.

Individuals with different background experience can receive different messages from the same sentence and be stimulated into thinking many different thoughts. Depending on the immediate circumstance and context, the words can also excite different responses. This very human situation highlights the difficulty of bridging the gap between our knowledge base and our understanding. A knowledge base of scientific and technological data can probably be constructed, but understanding, and especially if we want to link our understanding to the philosophical aspect of life, is far more elusive to being reduced systematically. Our experriences are built up over many years, and we, the human race, are now about 4,800 million strong. The sum total of our experience is such a colossal bag of tricks that it will probably defy any attempt to reduce it and thereby change us into a group of homogeneous thinking machines. We seem to have a will to make our contribution to society individually in one way or another. This reduction to sameness seems to work against that will. We are too clever to fall into this trap. In spite of our worry of being drowned in the flood of data, information, or knowledge, we are more likely to seize the opportunities that this abundance of knowledge creates and make strides towards data reduction, only to start anew from a more manageable set of newly ordered disciplines from which to begin our creative process again.

Chapter 4

From Transistor to VLSI

The transistor was a technological invention which opened the door to the information society. Tracing its development is important to understanding how the business world dealt with this landmark invention. The impact of the transistor was immense. The making and using of transistors caused the rise and fall of many businesses.

Transistors were preceded by vacuum tubes; vacuum tubes were the beginning of our electronic age. When Lee de Forest invented the triode, a vacuum tube with three electrodes, a whole new world opened up, a world in which we could harness the electrons to help us. This was a technological development which linked many scientific advances together and allowed the practical usage of electromagnetic energy, particularly for signal processing and transmission purposes.

The triode has a cathode which emits electrons and an anode which collects them. The third electrode is called a grid, which is placed in between, but in close proximity to the cathode. The grid is a sieve which interrupts the electron flow from the cathode to the anode when it is biased to repel electrons, and enhances the electron flow when it is biased to attract electrons. The position of the grid enables weak signals applied to it to cause large changes in the electrons flowing from the cathode to the anode. By arranging the triode in a suitable circuit, the input signal can be amplified into a large output signal with little distortion and the circuit can respond at a speed of many millions of cycles per second. By arranging the output to be returned to the input, the circuit can be made to sustain continuous oscillation. Electromagnetic energy oscillating at a specific frequency can, thereby, be generated in this circuit, which is known as an oscillator. Thus, the triode allows direct current energy obtained from primary electricity generators to be converted to electromagnetic energy at different frequencies; it can also provide amplification for the signals.

Speech and sound in electrical signal form can then be transmitted over long distances with the help of amplifiers which boost the signal level whenever it, on account of transmission losses, becomes too low for detection. Furthermore, high-frequency electromagnetic energy can serve as a carrier of lower frequency signals which are super-imposed on the carrier through a process known as modulation. This process provides different ways to transmit a signal since electromagnetic energy at different frequencies propagates efficiently in different ways. For example, a carrier at one mega-Hertz (MHz) can be made to propagate omnidirectionally in free space and it can be received at many stations over a distance of tens of kilometers. It is conveniently used as a means of broadcasting in cities. Frequencies around 1 MHz are known as the medium waveband and are used by many radio stations. At the same time, 1 MHz can propagate along copper wires, acting as an information carrier. One hundred and twenty telephone signals can be accommodated on this carrier in such a way that all 120 telephone signals can be transmitted along the same wire simultaneously and separated at the receiving end. Obviously, this is 120 times more efficient than using one pair of wires for each telephone signal. An even more striking example is the use of a carrier at 100 million MHz. This carrier frequency corresponds to light waves. When propagated in an optical fiber, it can span long distances with only a few amplifiers. Over 200,000 separate telephone signals can be simultaneously transmitted by a single optical carrier along a fiber over many kilometers.

The impact of the triode was felt not only in the signal transmission area but also in the signal processing area. Two triodes arranged in a so-called flip-flop circuit act as a logic element with ON–OFF states. This allows the manipulation of electrical signals in pulsed form. Thus, triodes and their variants ushered in our digital electronic age. These devices allowed us to establish our worldwide telephone system, radio and radar systems and much more. During the 1940s, electronic computing machines were first designed with thousands of triodes. Here the limitations of the triode became all too apparent.

The triode uses a heating element to enhance the electron emission from the cathode materials. Two problems exist. One is the life of the cathode including the heating element; it is only several thousand hours. The other is the conversion efficiency. Considerable energy is needed for achieving the required electron emission. Much heat has to be dissipated in addition to the large amount of power needed to make the triode function. When thousands of these devices are to be used, the power and life problems suddenly become overwhelming. The first computer was a heavy consumer of power and was as hot as a furnace. The failure rate of the triodes was horrendous. On top of all this, the computer was not very powerful even if several thousand more triodes were used. Triodes and their deficiencies prompted the scientists and technologists to look for an ultimate three-terminal element which could amplify, was small, dissipated little energy and could respond to very high frequencies.

At that point in time, a variety of scientific and technological endeavors were making significant advances. The possibility of making an equivalent triode from semi-conductor material was recognized. Even though various advances were made in separate fields for a variety of reasons, and even though the invention was not exactly planned in an orderly fashion, the transistor was born.

Those working in the various fields, which later were found to be crucial for the transistor, were pursuing goals in many directions. Work in solid-state physics was directed towards gaining a better understanding of the properties of metals and insulators in crystalline and amorphous forms. The application of quantum mechanics to solid-state physics treated problems of the solid at a sub-atomic structural level. The hope was to obtain a way of describing the electronic behavior of materials better. In the course of these studies, a class of materials, called semi-conductors, was discovered. The simplest of such materials could be found in the Group VI elements in the periodic table, such as germanium and silicon. Normally, the material was an insulator with no electrons available for conduction, since the molecules were made with atoms whose four outer orbit electrons form a strong covalent bond with each other. However, if impurities of Group III or Group V compounds happened to be present, the material exhibited some conductivity; not as strong as a metal but more than an insulator. Hence, the name semi-conductor. The interesting thing which was discovered by chance was the presence of a rectifier action when the semi-conductor material was touched by a whisker of a wire of conducting material. At the contact, current can flow one way with ease but not in the reverse direction. The electron flow is unidirectional. This was recognized as significant by those working with vacuum tubes, since this unidirectional electron flow action resembled the flow of electrons from the cathode to the anode in a triode, which is also unidirectional.

Other areas of investigation were the purification of materials and crystal growth. Crystalline materials have served mankind for millenia as precious ornamental stones, as optical material capable of controlling lightwaves, and as mechanically strong materials for industry, etc. Purification of materials also has been pursued for a variety of reasons in the course of the development of chemistry and metallurgy. The identification of semi-conductor materials has prompted work in growing pure semi-conductor host materials to supplement naturally obtained germanium crystals found in mineral deposits.

William Schockley and a number of his colleagues at Bell Laboratories were working assiduously on projects leading to an understanding of the mechanism of the point-contact diode, which the whiskered germanium device was called. The paths to the eventual understanding of this mechanism were tortuous. Along the way, semi-conductors were better understood as made up of a host Group VI material plus a controlled amount of impurities known as dopants, and a p-type and n-type could be created by adding Group III and Group V elements respectively. The p-type acquires conduction due to the deficiency of an electron in satisfying the outer orbital and the n-type acquires it due to an excess of an electron in the same outer orbit. The crystalline material, with a purity greater than one part in 1,000,000,000 and with controlled dopants up to one part in 1,000 concentration, can provide semi-conductors with well-defined properties.

The p-type and n-type, when in contact, were found to have the rectifying property of a point-contact diode, but this time along the entire junction. This was named a junction diode. With this device in place, the prospect of creating a triode-equivalent rose substantially.

The steps towards achieving the junction diode involved making very significant advances in crystal growth technology and material purification and in methods of applying controlled amounts of dopents. It was a brilliant technological achievement. Coupled with the improved theoretical understanding of solid-state physics, including the all-important Band Theory, which explains how electrons behave within a crystalline material, the stage was set for the successful making of transistors.

When a sandwiched layer of p–n–p or n–p–n is made, the action of applying a reverse bias across one p–n junction followed by a forward bias (i.e., one junction is biased so that one direction of flow of electrons is enhanced and the other is discouraged), enables the three-terminal device to work as a triode. The intermediate region must be thin, just as in the case of the grid, to act as a sieve. The transistor turns out to be small and efficient. Furthermore, the voltage needed for its operation is a few volts instead of the nearly 100 volts which the triode must have. This came as a god-send for the electronics industry. All electronic equipment appeared to benefit in one way or another by incorporating the use of transistors. However, the vacuum-tube industry fought a strong rear-guard battle, and the replacement of tubes by transistors happened only gradually over many years. Industrial leaders, alas, took very cautious views on the potential of the transistor, which was regarded as a new toy from the research center with some unique advantages but generally was considered inferior to vacuum tubes in performance. Several large corporations with early research activities in this area were uncertain as to how to make the transistor a commercial proposition. The manufacturing technology and control were far outside their normal experience, and initial market demand was estimated to be relatively soft.

What history showed was a case of entrepreneurial success. A few small companies began to make transistors. Some Japanese companies saw the opportunity of creating a new product, the pocket radio receiver, using transistors in place of vacuum tubes and small dry batteries instead of AC mains as the power source. All at once, transistors were needed in the millions for new products to which only transistors could give birth.

In the meantime, the performance of transistors improved as materials, fabrication technologies and theoretical understanding continued to increase. The infrastructure for the semi-conductor industry with its requirements for high-purity chemicals, novel instrumentation for measurements of semi-conductor properties, such as the Hall effect, photo luminescence, etc. began to appear. Germanium devices were soon supplemented by silicon devices. Single crystals of larger and larger dimensions with low-defect density and with well-controlled crystal orientation started to become available. Photolithographic techniques enabled large numbers of transistors to be made simultaneously. Long lines of assembly personnel peering under microscopes made separate devices from a silicon wafer with these separate devices made on it through the use of lithographic masks and photo-resist materials that allow separate processes to be performed on a wafer. Suddenly, the price of a transistor was well below the equivalent cost of a vacuum-tube device. More and more devices could be incorporated to achieve better and/or different performance in various types of equipment.

The opportunities for using transistors increased while the performance of transistors also made steady improvement. Computers involving thousands of transistors became a reality and at attractive costs. More powerful computers with hundred thousands or millions of transistors can be envisaged. New companies began to appear as computer makers for special and big mainframe machines. The definition of the desirable performances of the transistors is towards an ultimate device of very small size, with practically no dissipation and capable of very high speed. Today, the ultimate performance is beginning to be influenced by fundamental limits of physics, but a transistor occupying an area of a wafer of less than $0.1 \times 0.1 \ \mu m^2$ can be envisaged. A transistor pair for switching can operate with very much less than 1 pJ of energy and can have an operating speed approaching 100 GHz.

The computer makers saw the transistors as logic elements and as fast memories using ON/OFF as memory states. They also discovered very rapidly that the major problems of using the many transistors that were needed to make powerful digital computers were power dissipation, packaging and interconnection. Since transistors could be made on a silicon wafer and then be diced into individual units, why could they not be made a group at a time with interconnections provided? This way, a larger unit for some specific function could be made in an integrated form. These could be diced into separate units and packaged with a certain number of interconnection output leads. The concept was attractive and the required technological progress was made. Thus, the integrated circuit or IC came into existence.

If in the 1940s the inventors of transistors or the transistor users were asked whether they could envisage making IC's or would be needing IC's, the answers would probably be "no." They could not see the vast potential IC's would eventually bring, but they could see the enormous complications of building two transistors side-by-side with no mutual interference when a single transistor was already a challenge. Hence, the development path of transistors moved along initially in the direction of improving device characteristics towards high frequency and/or high power capabilities. These devices were mainly envisaged as vacuum tube replacements. However, the boom of transistors actually came from products for which transistors served as the enabling technology.

Integrated circuits were a solution to a problem identified by the computer makers. The progression in this development of transistors was through medium-scale integration (MSI), large-scale integration (LSI), very-large-scale integration (VLSI), ultra-large-scale integration (ULSI) and wafer-scale integration (WSI). The descriptive terms have no strict quantitative measures. VLSI chips probably started with a 10,000 transistor chip, interconnected and partitioned, to perform a specific function, while ultra-large-scale integrated circuits probably started with one million transistor chips. What was not entirely expected was that this "solution to a problem" could turn out to be a starting point for much larger business opportunities. The integrated microcircuit, in the form of what is now called a microprocessor, is a new system building-block which promises to open the way to building systems and equipment with memory and control reminiscent of human intelligence.

The success in producing integrated circuits was due to major technological advances made in a large number of areas. It has been mentioned that lithographic techniques are used for discrete transistor production. This was and is a key technology area.

Integrated circuits, so far, are mainly fabricated in a planar configuration. Devices and interconnections are made on a planar substrate using several layers of different materials fabricated one on top of the other. The sandwiched structure is designed to function as a transistor. By using lithographic techniques, these layers are fabricated only where they are to be located. Other layers serving different roles are also fabricated. These include conductors for interconnecting the transistors in a defined pattern and oxide layers for isolation and passivation coating. For a complex structure some ten or more masks are used for creating the necessary structures on the wafer.

Lithography is a pattern-making process. The pattern is often hand drawn and then reduced photographically, and a mask is produced. This mask is then projected on to the semi-conductor wafer over which a photo-sensitive material known as photo-resist has been applied. The projected pattern is retained as the unwanted portion of the photo-resist is removed through etching. The specific layer to be fabricated is then erected on the wafer through material deposition or diffusion. Successive layers are made the same way.

The techniques for producing precision patterns, for applying photo-resists uniformly over a wafer, for alignment of successive masks and for making precision narrow lines turned out to be non-trivial tasks which took time and effort for successful implementation. A mask aligner is still a very high-cost item, especially one for making devices with small features.

As the feature size of the devices gets into the micrometer order region, mask-making requires photographic techniques with the use of very short wavelength light or the use of electron beams. Hence, VLSI circuits became feasible only recently, when ultra-violet lithography and electron-beam lithography had been sufficiently well developed for industrial usage.

Epitaxy is the growth of single-crystal semi-conductor material on top of a semi-conductor substrate material. This branch of technology has made very significant progress. For silicon devices this technique is not needed since the junction type of devices made with layers of p and n doped silicon were achieved through a diffusion process. The metal-oxide-silicon (MOS) transistors, consisting of an oxide layer and then a metallic layer on top of a silicon substrate, can be done through a simple deposition process coupled with the oxidation of the silicon surface.

Epitaxy, however, is extending the material system suitable for transistor making to beyond germanium and silicon to compound semi-conductors such as gallium arsenide. The advantages of such material over silicon includes higher temperature capabilities and high electron mobility which can be translated into higher frequency and higher power devices.

Crystal growth technology has resulted in the availability of large single crystal wafers with a high degree of uniformity and very low-defect density. This allows a large number of devices in IC form to be fabricated on a single substrate, thereby maintaining the advantages of the single transistor-making days of being able to process one wafer to obtain a large number of devices. A step-and-repeat system allows masks to be projected repeatedly over the entire wafer without loss of the registration accuracy essential when multiple layers must be created.

If the entire wafer can be used as a single device for applications where many IC's must be used, then the interconnections can be internal to the wafer and total circuit reliability may also be improved.

Cleanliness is also a technology. The IC's with device feature sizes comparable to the size of dust particles must be made in very clean areas which must be dust free and humidity-and-temperature-controlled. Advances in air-filter design, air-conditioning and air-flow control enable so-called class ten cleanliness to be achieved. This means that an average of ten dust particles, submicron in size, will exist in a cubic foot of air. Operators in the clean area must wear dust-free overalls, and the number of operators should be kept to a minimum.

The preparation of semi-conductor material included as a step the washing and cleaning of the surface. This process usually involves the use of high-purity water which has been de-ionized to a high resis-tivity and is dust free. The maintenance of pure water is complex since the filters are not effective against organic moleculars such as algae.

The cleanliness requirement for wafer-scale integration and ultra-large-scale integration probably will demand a humanless factory. Sophisticated automation is involved.

Clearly, a multiplicity of technologies are involved in supporting the advances in IC capabilities. It is important to note the impact on business. The resources expended in R&D are huge. These are recouped through many channels. The indirect businesses are the making and selling of sophisticated scientific instruments such as electron microscopes and spectrometers and specialized production equipment such as mask aligners, wafer-processing furnaces and clean rooms. The most direct business is in semi-conductor crystals, processing chemicals, and, of course, the semi-conductor devices in a variety of generic IC forms. Some R&D cost is paid by users who need the semi-conductor products in tailor-made forms. This huge industry faces a difficult challenge. The investment needed to establish a new entity is large. Even the established companies find the cost of introducing new generic IC products a time-consuming and a high-risk endeavor. The cause of both can be traced to the status of the technology and the market.

IC's were recognized as a way to achieve larger and faster computers, and the initiative came from the computer industry. Transistors were used extensively to achieve the logic circuits needed within the computer. Fast memory called Random Access Memories (RAM) was also an important element. The computer industry used this in very large quantities; hence, the cost per chip decreased rapidly. All of a sudden these chips were affordable by everyone, even for those designing simple controls for domestic appliances. At the same time, the chip makers had found ways to make a more complete circuit on a single chip. The microprocessor chip with a memory, arithmetic unit, and input/output control became a stand-alone component which could be considered as a new system building-block. This chip was also a low-cost component since it was made in the millions. With technological advances, microprocessors of greater power and speed came on the market in quick succession. The complexity of the chip was measured in the hundreds of thousands of transistors.

The features which can be realized in a microprocessor or a chip with several hundreds of thousands of transistors are almost unlimited. The design task is so complex that the time needed for the introduction of a new microprocessor is several years. The product life at the same time could be as short as a year or two. The onus on the manufacturer of such a product is very big, particularly for a newcomer.

Here is a clear case of the type of difficulty, technology can bring to a market. It is true that the new microprocessor is a viable product and will be snapped up by computer makers. It is also true that technology can make such a product. Nevertheless, it is a big boy's game where the risks and rewards are very high. Meanwhile the computer industry is also caught in this high-stake game, as will be described in the next chapter.

From the viewpoint of the makers of other products, transistors and IC's have vastly expanded the scope of system design. In consumer products, transistors, as noted earlier, introduced pocket radios. Home entertainment sets have all been transistorized, ranging from tape recorders to TV sets. Recently, digital TV sets using a set of custom-made IC's came onn the market with distinct feature advantages. In professional equipment, the use of IC's is extensive, particularly for telecommunications. Telecommunications, which used to do signal processing on an analog form, has now turned almost completely to digital techniques. The economics of digital systems is the overwhelming reason for this shift. If the transistor had not been invented, this would not be possible. For those particularly interested in understanding the impact of technology on business, a comment on two other related technologies is in order. The telecommunication network became a wholly digital system due to the work of Shannon, who made it clear that analog signals, such as speech, can be precisely reconstructed from its digital form. The other work is due to Reeves, who invented the pulse-code-modulation (PCM) scheme which encoded digital signals in a code of 1's and 0's only. This PCM signal can, therefore, be handled with ease by transistor circuits.

The low-cost, relatively low-performance IC's are enabling automatic controls with simulated intelligence to be installed on any appliance. Microwave ovens with programmed cooking schedules and washing machines with several selections of washing cycles are typical examples. Transistors are really touching every phase of our life. Their potential impact in the future is even more mind-boggling.

An IC chip of one million transistors is envisaged as sufficient for making a speech recognition unit. This unit would be able to understand voice commands and to translate them into action. Already pilots are testing out such devices in high-performance aircraft so that they can order actions when their hands, feet and eyes are engaged with other actions. Voice-command dialing of telephones has been demonstrated. The caller just says the name or the number he wishes to call and this unit will translate his voice into the dialing code which initiates the call. In the future, voice recognition can be used as a security check since voice signatures of individuals are just as distinct as fingerprints.

An IC chip of four million transistors is envisaged as sufficient for making a pattern-recognition unit. This is a direct assault on extending our vision-processing ability. The application potentials are unlimited.

The transistor, which had a small beginning as a replacement for a vacuum tube, has made a very significant impact on our society. It created a computer industry and made the telecommunication network go digital. In fact, it has opened the way for computers and telecommunications to merge into an information network which is highly relevant to the needs of our age.

The future IC's are promising to enhance our signal-processing capability by linking our speech and vision more directly into our information network. This will greatly simplify the input/output problems between man and machines.

The transistor is not without basic limitations. Its ON/OFF characteristic is operating in a one-dimensional (1-D) world. The digital characteristics are powerful, but when two-dimensional (2-D) or three-dimensional (3-D) signals are to be processed, it may not be the most ideal way. The transistor also has an upper-frequency limit for its speed of operation. This limits the absolute speed on which a 1-D pulse train can be processed. Hence, other more natural 2-D and 3-D signal-processing techniques, such as those which will be discussed in Chapter 5, could come forth to replace some of the roles of the ubiquitous transistors.

Probably the impact of the transistor on business is a good indication of the way in which technologies with broad applications can perform. The transistor created its own industries. It fostered the existence of relevant support industries which enabled transistors to be made and improved. It generated industries which use the functionality of the transistor. Without transistors there would be no computers. But if computers were not destined to play a significant role in our daily lives, then even with the transistor, we would not have had computers. Technology is a means to make certain things happen to fulfill our needs.

Chapter 5

From the Abacus to Computer

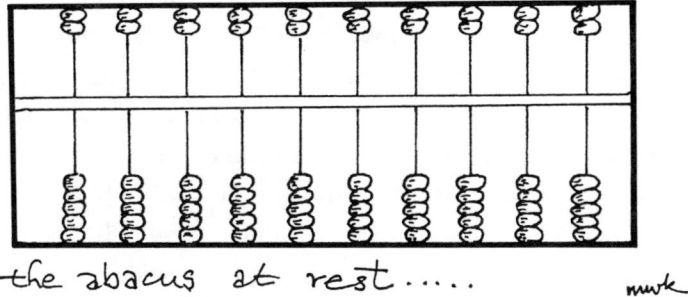

the abacus at rest.....   mwk

From the abacus to computers, man seeks computational aids. The impact of technology on the development of computational aids is fascinating. The abacus survived over 5,000 years of usage. The mechanical calculators and slide rules lasted one and a half centuries, while electronic calculators and computers only appeared about thirty years ago. Although computers are very recent, they are broadening their usage from calculations into reasoning, far-removed from mere computation.

Somehow counting is an indispensable part of our life. We count the number of fingers and toes the baby has when it is born to make sure that all ten of them are present, no more, no less. We count out time in minutes or seconds when we are anxious, in years when we are lamenting the passage of our youth. We count the change the supermarket cashier gives us after we pay our bill. We count our blessings when we feel grateful. Life is simply full of counting, but we seldom associate counting as a business unless we are reminded that accountants make their living counting for us. In fact, counting is so deeply intertwined with our life that the story "from the abacus to computers" can bring out clearly how the technology of counting is responsible for the development of our commerce and civilization.

The abacus is a counting instrument. In its original form it probably precedes the concept of numbers. A bead represents one, and another bead represents another one. Putting the two together makes two "ones." Putting a few of them together makes many "ones." The concept of none, one and many gradually leads to one-to-one representation and a big "one" to many small "ones" concept. It is not hard to imagine that before long our prehistoric forefathers somehow found the way to understand that a pebble can represent 5 beans so that if we want to indicate 10 beans we can say 2 pebbles. While the numbers up to 10 are enumerable with our fingers, the idea of many 10's by beans placed in another area must have been relatively slow to be appreciated. Anyhow, the abacus with lower beads representing "1's" and the upper beads representing "5's" and the adjacent column representing a multiple factor of 10 came into existence after the decimal number system was reasonably well established.

The abacus is a portable, simple easily-constructed instrument which permits easy recording and erasing of numbers and, with a few simple rules of manipulation, it can do sums, differences, multiplication and division. Basically, the abacus uses movable beads to represent numbers. All beads on the abacus are threaded along adjacently placed stems which are mounted perpendicular to an upper, a lower and a partition bar. In each column two beads are on top and five beads are in the lower part of the stem. To start computation, all beads must be placed away from the partition bar between the upper and lower regions such that upper beads are against the upper bar and lower beads are against the lower bar. It is instructive to note a simple rule associated with addition to see that the computation can be carried out easily by a person without any knowledge of the theory of addition or numbers.

The rules to keep in mind for calculations on the abacus are uncomplicated. Whenever all five beads are in the up position in the lower column, they can be returned down to the zero position and replaced by bringing down one of the beads in the upper section of the same column. Whenever both of the upper beads are already down in any column, they can be returned up to the zero position and replaced by putting up one bead from the adjacent left lower column. The user can arbitrarily choose a column as the digits column; then the columns to the right are decimal places decreasing by orders of ten and, of course, to the left are columns increasing by orders of ten. The reader can experiment for himself following these rules for both addition and subtraction. Naturally, multiplication is really addition and division is subtraction. The answers can be read

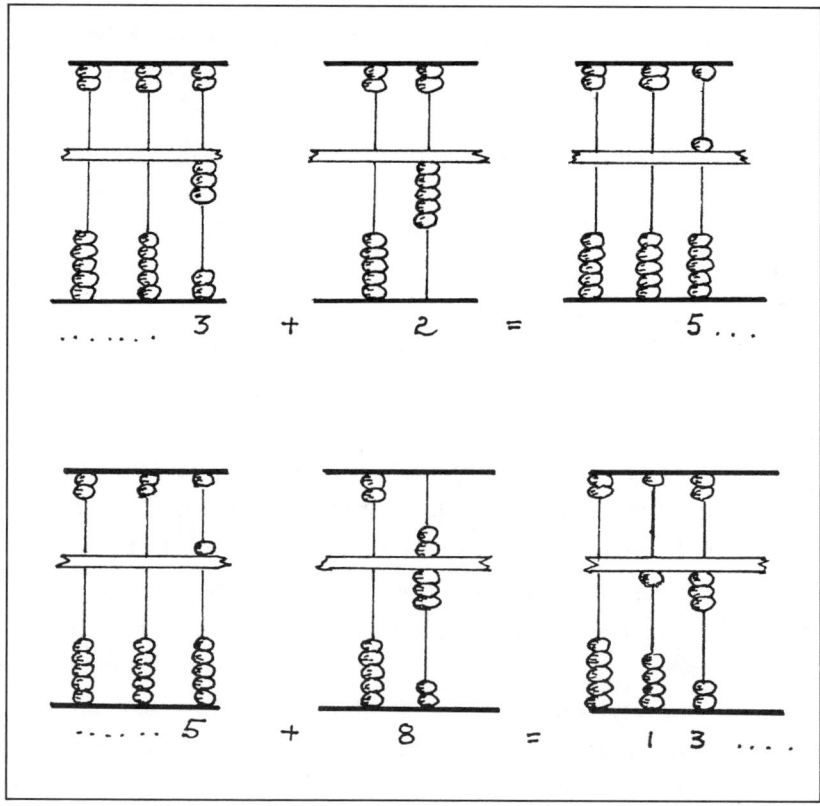

off exactly in the familiar decimal system. With such a long history of abacus usage, the Chinese have developed a standard ritual of finger movements, together with rhymes memorized in their youth, like music to accompany the dance of the figures.

These rules make computation highly mechanical, and to this day a skillful abacus operator can out-perform a mechanical calculator on any computation or a digital pocket calculator on addition and even on simple multiplications.

The abacus serves as a counting instrument to this day mainly in China and Japan. It must rank as one of the longest-run products of all times. The modern abacus differs little in design, except perhaps in the material used for its construction. New abacuses can be made in plastics, as well as in traditional wood and bamboo.

The invention of the abacus as a computational instrument met our needs in many ways. First, it is a teaching tool which permits a decimal system to be taught with visual and conceptual clarity. Secondly, it allows computation to be mechanically carried out and it has erasable storage of intermediate and final results. Thirdly, it is sufficiently powerful to deal with the day-to-day computations encountered by households, shops and banks. Fourthly, it is as powerful as any mechanical decimal-number calculator, but it is much cheaper and easier to maintain. It is not surprising that the abacus has such longevity as a product and that it has served us well.

Gradually, as our computational requirements increased, more powerful aids were found to be necessary. Even then, the abacus actually provided some useful hints in the design of mechanical calculators and even the digital computer. The mechanical calculators and cash registers work on the same principle as the abacus, except that the numbers are represented by gear wheels whose mechanical linkage is such that decimal numbers can be translated into the mechanical movement of wheel and gear ratios. These machines are driven manually or by electrical motors. Besides computation, the printing out of the numbers during and after computation are also provided, so that these machines became accounting machines for use by accountants and bank clerks, and cash registers for use at every shop. The calculating machines became the basis of a large business.

The competing manufacturers introduced machines with special features. For cash registers a convenient high-speed data entry was found to be important; for accounting machines, convenient functions such as percentages and storage of intermediate results were welcomed by the users. The size, features, appearance, convenience, reliability, and even printout formats were all product-differentiating features. No one, however, envisaged cash registers as part of sales machines which could be linked with inventory control or with electronic input facilities.

On the scientific and technological front, the demand for computations is in many forms, including the calculation of the numerical values of functions such as sine, cosine, and tangent for trigonometric tables, numerical solutions of equations and integrals, and mathematical analysis. The invention of the logarithm led to the invention of the slide rule. This is an instrument which essentially allows additions to be made in a geometric way. If one linear scale slides over another, the two numbers represented by the uniform calibration on both scales can be added by bringing the 0 of the sliding scale onto the first number and reading off the sum under the second number. Since the logarithm converts multiplication to addition and division to subtraction, the slide rule can suitably be calibrated in a logarithmic scale and, thereby, permit multiplication to be performed on the slide rule. Furthermore, with the use of a moving cursor and other scales, the slide rule can be used to compute trigonometric and exponential functions. It became the hand tool of engineers who needed to do a lot of computation but who were not unduly concerned about getting results accurate to many decimal places. The manufacture of slide rules became a large industry, but it died with the coming of the all-function pocket calculators. The rise and fall of the slide rule is an example of a product born out of new knowledge and technology and which died because of another technological advance.

The scientific knowledge of logarithms and the technological knowledge of precision calibration of rulers were responsible for the success of bringing slide-rule products into existence. Initially, companies engaged in stationery products, particularly those producing rulers, became interested in this mass product for millions of engineers and university students. Slide rules for jacket pockets, for desks, with many functions, or with few functions, appeared in a dazzling array over a period of about twenty years. Books on how to use slide rules, slide rules with magnifying sensors and even slide rules with mechanical calculators all flourished for a while. The competition was on price and features.

Basically the demand was overwhelming and the product sold well. Slide rules fulfilled a real need and were well accepted by the peer groups. The market did reach saturation towards the end. Manufacturers resorted to incorporating features, which were seldom used, as sales gimmicks. Even then, the decline of this product was not expected. The end came with great suddenness when the electronic calculators arrived. This aspect will be taken up a little later. The slide rule was a scientific tool and was the start of computation known later as analog computing. It utilized an analog method to arrive at the answer. The slide rule uses the properties of logarithmic functions to make multiplication and division a linear process.

From slide rules and calculating machines, theoreticians pondered on the significance of computability. Turing, a mathematician, put forward a theorem about computability which suggested later to Von Neumann and others methods for making a computer based on binary numbers. The link between the abacus, slide rules, adding machines and the computer is traceable, but this is not what we need to discuss. Before moving to electronic digital computers, it is important to point out that the early computational machines were intimately human related. The man-machine interface was direct and simple. In fact, people loved the feel of the abacus and the slide rule.

The digital computer, however, was altogether a different thing.

The early versions were large and awe-inspiring. Communication between man and the machine was through symbolic instructions with no reference whatsoever to the human experience of computation. It conjured up the image of a new brain threatening our mere existence. Initially it was pitifully limited in performance, even though it could do a single addition at the seemingly astonishingly high speed of less than a thousandth of a second.

The digital computer designed by Von Neumann is conceptually simple. It has a central processing unit (CPU) which allows binary arithmetic of additions to be performed, using an electronic circuit known as shift-registers, and sequential execution of control instructions. It has a digital signal store and accepts signal input in the form of a sequence of electrical impulses coded as instructions and data. The instructions and data are stored and brought out one by one into the CPU for execution and processing. The output is stored and made available to drive output machines such as printers. It is a sequential machine which works on one instruction at a time. The throughput is, therefore, dependent on how fast a single instruction is executed.

With the use of electronic circuits the time needed to perform one instruction is seen to be short, so that at least thousands of instructions can be executed per second. The promises of the computer appeared very attractive. Despite technological difficulties, the first electronic computer using triode vacuum tubes as switching elements capable of handling binary signals was made for experimental purposes. As described in the previous chapter, this computer used too much power. The invention of transistors resolved this difficulty and enabled digital computers to be made as marketable products.

At first the power of the computer was not recognized or commercially exploited. Obviously an electronic computer could do computation, but a computer capable of making useful scientific computations was rather hard to visualize. A computer capable of helping to run a business could be envisaged. Again the design of such a computer was a tough problem. A computer was also an excellent control machine, but few people had the foresight to envisage its effective usage. The time for the widespread use of computers had not yet arrived.

Perhaps it was the urgent need of the scientific and technological community to have some powerful machine to do computation, or perhaps it was the sheer enthusiasm of the computer designers. The net result was the successful design and making of a computer product for scientific computation. It was an electronic equivalent of a mechanical calculator that could work at least a thousand times faster.

The early computer makers had to overcome many technological problems. The transistors were a must. They permitted power-efficient operation and removed some of the most serious problems of heat dissipation from the electronic circuits. Even more pertinent were the small dimensions of the transistor which allowed the size of the computer to be reduced for convenient installation in a room. The increased reliability helped to make the machine maintainable for dependable usage. All these were conditions which had to be met before the computer could be marketable as a product.

The memory unit was a significant challenge. The initial solution was the magnetic drum with multiple read and write heads for quick records retrieval and fast write, respectively. This was a feat of engineering. The cylindrical drum was made of a thermally stable metal and coated with a ferromagnetic film. In operation the drum, with a diameter of around 20 cm and a height of about 50 cm, had to rotate at speeds in the order of at least 10,000 rpm. The size of the drum and the rotating speed governed the access time to the memory store and the capacity of the store. However, the precision requirements became very tough to meet. The magnetic drum was probably the most delicate part of the machine. It needed a temperature-stable environment and a few minutes of running time until stable operation could be reached.

The input/output electronics were relatively simple. They consisted of coding an alpha-numeric set of symbols into equivalent binary codes. At that time the telegraphic coding was well established and new codes more appropriate for binary representation were generated. At the same time, the typewriter mechanism was there to be used. Thus, the input to the computer was via a typewriter which converted the manually inputted symbols, representing instructions and data, into electrical inputs into the machine. The output was a stream of electrical impulses which were used to activate typewriter keys for a printed output or to activate a cathode ray tube (CRT) for a display on a screen.

The CRT was a high-technology invention of great ingenuity and significance. It was derived from the triode, but it used the electrons for a new purpose. The electrons from the cathode, controlled by the grid, were accelerated by a series of anodes and were shaped into an electron beam by the use of an electric or a magnetic field. This beam was made to strike a screen. The energy from the high-speed electrons excited the phosphor material on the screen and caused the material to emit energy in the form of visible light. This invention was a remarkable accomplishment in the application of knowledge in physics. It involved the generation of electrons by using heat to release the electrons from materials with low work function (a term used to describe how strongly electrons are attached to materials); the control and shaping of the free electrons by an electric and/or a magnetic field as predicted by the theory of electromagnetism; the evacuation of the region in which electrons traveled so that electrons would not collide with obstacles in the form of molecules; and the conversion of the kinetic energy of the fast-moving electrons to excite electrons within the phosphor so that visible light was generated. The theory of phosphorescence was postulated by Einstein not many years before the CRT was invented. Altogether, the CRT was so complex that few would give it a chance for mass usage. Yet it not only served well as a high-speed screen for computers; it also created at least two major industries on its own. One was in the electronic instruments industry. The CRT is a part of practically every high-speed electronic test instrument. The other is in the far larger industry of television sets. The CRT's in TV sets eventually reached such a height of engineering achievement that the tubes with rectangular screen size up to 70 cm in diagonal length could be made to display full color pictures. Three different types of phosphors are used, each emitting a primary color. Each picture element contains one dot each of these three phosphors. Over one million picture elements are arranged in precise rows and columns to cover the entire screen. Such tubes are produced on a fully automated assembly line.

This is a highly instructive example of technology creating a key component which enabled other new industries to come into existence. It also shows how human ingenuity turned knowledge into practice.

Coming back from this CRT diversion, the last, but not the least, problem in the making of a computer was the design and implementation of the control function. This could be implemented by specific electronic circuits which generate dedicated* control instructions in a stream of electronic impulses, or by a set of electronic circuits generating instructions which form a basic language. More complex instructions can be composed from this basic language. The dedicated instructions generated by a specific circuit were referred to as hardware programming, and the language style instruction was referred to as software. For example, a hardware program could be made for making matrix multiplication. An external action such as the pushing of a button is involved to initiate this program.

A hardware-generated instruction is commonly used in electronic pocket calculators. The software equivalent operation involved the writing of the operations to be done in the instruction language. This set of instructions is entered into the computer. The control sees these instructions and makes up the electronic instructions equivalent to that generated by the previous dedicated hardware. Effectively, there is a trade-off situation of making dedicated hardware or instruction hardware. However, this is a very significant trade-off. The software

----

* "Dedicated" is a technical jargon meaning "specially assigned."

can be made extremely powerful if the basic instruction set is well designed. It really corresponds to language development with a limited set of vocabulary. In English, a 500-word set could convey a good many meanings. The computer language is simpler and less powerful. Usually, a set of fifty logical statements allows a useful language to be generated. The flexibility of the usage of language tends to exceed the power of dedicated hardware. Hence, software/hardware is a complex trade-off situation. Software allows less hardware to be needed within a computer and hence reduces the equipment cost. However, dedicated hardware allows faster and more reliable operation and also permits more powerful software schemes to be generated. Some additional problems actually arise due to the nature of the software. Since software resembles a language and since language usually permits more than one way of usage, computer instructions in software form tend to be written by individuals to suit their own tastes. This has resulted in two problems; one is the difficulty of reading a software instruction set, called a program, prepared by others, and the other is the temptation of trying to use the language too cleverly in an effort to reduce the number of instructions. This tends to make the program difficult to analyze, just as a student majoring in English would find difficulty in trying to analyze a beautiful sentence in an essay into its grammatical structure. In fact, software is a significant area of development and research in its own right, and it is the basis of a separate industry. On the other hand, computers should of course be developed with the software and hardware trade-off constantly in mind.

The computer is clearly a product of a very high order of complexity and cannot be developed without the use of many supporting technologies, as well as the use of new techniques special to computers. With a great deal of labor of love and inspiration, the first computer product met the approval of the scientific community. This computational machine was capable of doing one thousand man-days of work in one day. A clamor for larger and faster machines soon followed.

The story of the development of transistors in integrated circuit form has already been told in the previous chapter. This is the enabling technology which is needed for building computers. The IC's were not only pushed into existence by the computer industry, but were also instrumental in the development of many new industries, as discussed earlier. On the computer scene a new industry of electronic calculators was created. Again, several technological advances enabled the calculator industry to take off. These were the IC's themselves, the development of longer-life and smaller batteries, and the power efficient alfa-numeric displays that initially were gas-discharge luminescent cells and later were light-emitting diodes and liquid crystals. The first pocket calculators could only do simple arithmetic of addition, subtraction, multiplication and division and were larger than ideal. They made the coat pocket bulge unacceptably. Within a few years a range of calculators with improved performance and reduced size flooded the market. The mass introduction made the price of the calculators low enough for most people's budget. This was welcomed by persons who now could by-pass learning mental arithmetic. In fact, the hand-held calculator forced educationists to take another look at the real value of learning multiplication and long division in elementary schools. The calculator challenged the long traditions of learning the 3 R's in school in a fundamental way.

Should our children be blind to the joy of mentally playing with numbers? Should the parents be afraid that punching buttons will result in mental degeneracy? The answer to both questions is probably negative. We'll never cease to be excited by the beauty of number relationships, but we can easily accept that the tedium of sheer number crunching should be avoided.

The business of electronic calculators taught us an important lesson. The biggest winner was the Japanese industry, who used this opportunity as an effective step in learning how to mass-produce a rapidly changing product, how to market and distribute such a product, and how to meet different needs with one product. Calculators with simple functions can be made as give-away presents at an extremely low cost or as specialized products which people may buy for the convenience of having a calculator always at hand. Credit-card thin calculators and calculators incorporated in watches are two such examples. More sophisticated calculators with simple mathematical functions are intended for school children, and those with full mathematical functions are for university students and the professional engineer. These, as noted earlier, caused the demise of the slide rule. At the other extreme end of this scale, calculators with printer output and programmability appeared. These types of calculators are encroaching on the realms of general purpose computers. The dividing point where the calculator stops and the computer begins will never be clear but, from a business viewpoint, the personal computer is competing with the upper range of calculators. What we can learn from this is the importance of recognizing that high-technology products encourage fast obsolescence, broader varieties and narrower windows of opportunity. This looks simple and attractive, but the vastness of choice and the shortness of time to identify and tailor the product for specific markets make the successful operation of a business one of the major challenges of our time. This point is expanded by examples and is explained and emphasized throughout this book.

The scientific computer, in the meantime, has progressed steadily. The earlier software languages gave way to a few powerful and more standardized languages such as FORTRAN. The recognition that the computer should be a good organizer of simple functions such as payroll and inventory generated many business applications. The business software language of COBOL was introduced. The computer operation became streamlined. Different users could access the machines by submitting their work to computer-center personnel, who operated the machine so that long programs could be run at off-peak hours and all users could be kept happy. The preparation of programs in a form convenient for batch feeding into the computer became common. Faster output machinery was also designed so that printouts could be typed line by line or page by page instead of character by character. All this made the computer industry expand and prosper. The computer room also became a consumer of paper with a voracious appetite. Engineers' desks often became buried in stacks of computer printouts of which only one or two pages needed to be consulted. Bank vaults are full of computer-generated data which must be destroyed after a regulation period to make way for new data. In fact, at one time the forestry commissions were worried about the dramatic increase in paper consumption, and the paper industry worried by this situation advocated the recycling of the used paper. Thus a new business to deal with paper recycling was born.

The pressure to have individual terminals to access the computer and its stored data increased. Time-sharing machines emerged as the next hierarchy of computers. At the same time the telecommunication industry also discovered that computers were good as basic machines to provide storage and forward message delivery, a precursor to the electronic mail. Computer makers were quick to respond to that need. Specialized computers for data handling also became popular. Multiple interactive terminals provided time-sharing operations. The speed of operation of some computers began to approach one million instructions per second (1 MIP). The computer industry started with notions to replace cash-registers, but no computer in cash register form has emerged as a product. Instead, the mainframe computers became larger and more powerful.

As machines become more powerful and the range of applications broadens, the need to have a good operating system within the computer increases. These operating systems are software, internal to the machine, which permit the computer to perform efficiently in a large variety of modes. The development of the operating-system software was a nightmare for the computer companies. At one time this famous IBM story happened. The software package became so large that the interaction of the large number of people working on it became too loose, with the result that as more effort was applied, less progress was achieved. Eventually this problem was solved largely by applying engineering disciplines. Software development from that time underwent a significant change from essay writing to becoming an engineering endeavor with strict disciplines.

In the course of the development of computers, IC's were also developed for other uses, such as a radio on a chip, a microprocessor or a TV receiver. Now some IC's can accommodate a complete computer on a chip. Moreover, the power of such a single-chip computer rivals that of a mainframe computer which used to occupy a whole room. It can work at speeds approaching those of the best high-speed machine available less than ten years ago. This IC chip created the personal-computer business.

Personal computers (PC's) became popular at once. People imagined a whole host of possibilities to which they could put the computer to use. The PC's can organize our finances, file our correspondence, be used as an electronic memory typewriter with editing capabilities, provide video-game entertainment, and above all can teach children to be computer compatible. The market is flooded with PC's of different types to cater to a number of users. There are low-cost computers which use home TV sets as a display at a price tag from $100 upwards. There are computers for small businesses, for schools and for anyone who thinks he can benefit from a computer. These PC's represent a significant investment of between $1,000 and $2,000. There are the high-performance PC's for the professionals, with features that include higher speed, larger memory store and a wider range of language capabilities. Sometimes they come with networking capabilities. At the same time packaged software provides on-tap facilities to the user, such as balance-sheet computation, all-purpose word processing, inventory control, etc. Users need not worry about learning how to program computers; yet they can still derive much benefit from them.

The PC business started with a bang. In some ways the PC is an extension of the calculator, grown to be an all-purpose machine with much more to offer than a dedicated calculator. In fact, the PC significantly affected the calculator market even though only a very few PC's were bought as calculators. This generated a software business since PC's need packaged software for all sorts of purposes. The making of software is like making a best-seller pop-music record. The program comes on a floppy disc just like record. Like pop records, many are made but only a few make it to the top. In other words, software is generated profusely, but only a few programs sell well. In general, software is written for a specific machine and is not usable on any other machine. Hence, there is pressure for PC's to be designed to be software compatible with the machine having the largest number of good software programs, even though most people will use such software infrequently.

In parallel with the PC development, computer techniques have been applied to word-processors and computer-aided design tools. Typewriters were transformed into machines with memories. Then the word-processor was developed by computer companies into a super-memory typewriter with electronic display and on-line editing capabilities. The improvement in printer technologies also allowed the word processor to have word font selection, mathematical symbol and layout capabilities. The word processors caught the immediate fancy of office secretaries as well as bosses, since the text can be edited without the dire consequences of a total retype. The process, however, is complex. First of all, the secretaries have to learn how to use this much more complex machine. Next, companies with computers find the justification to extend their computing facility to include word processing easier than buying new word-processing equipment. This resulted in companies with different units at separate locations opting for incompatible word-processing facilities. It created an curious industry-wide situation. Secretaries were trained over and over again on different word-processors. Documents made on one could not be transferred to others. The big hope of an all-electronic business world where documents and graphics from different companies and offices could be interchangeably processed is stymied by the lack of equipment compatibility. This is not a surprising situation. Nor should it cause undue alarm. It should serve as a lesson to note that an ideal solution takes time to evolve. Partial solutions will have to be used to gain partial advantages. A job is already well done if a partial solution is achieved.

No sooner had the dedicated word processors been introduced than the PC's with word-processing software began encroaching into the word-processing market. The price of the PC is comparable to a dedicated word processor such that PC's could be used economically solely as a word processor, even though it is capable of doing many other things. The basic PC can be considered as a generic product base. Thus, an important debate confronts the manufacturers and users alike: should they make/use dedicated products or generic ones?

The computer-aided design (CAD) area is even more complicated than the word-processing area. CAD for mechanical design and architectural plans have been in use for quite a time already. These provide checking for accuracy and design correctness based on some design rules. Final drawings and part lists are also provided. Obviously, these are specialized facilities designed to meet specific applications. The CAD tools have created business for tool producers and tool users, as well as for intermediaries to find the right tools for their clients. This field is highly technology driven. It is expected that more generic and more powerful tools often called workstations, will be forthcoming based on better databases, more powerful computers and better data-processing facilities. As indicated in Chapter 6, these facilities can be distributed along an information network and become part of the information service industry.

The integrated-circuit design tools are important for designers of complex IC's. In fact, very-large-scale IC's (VLSI) with thousands to millions of transistors cannot be designed without CAD tools of some sort. The design possibilities make optimization difficult. A company needing a certain class of circuits is likely to benefit most from a CAD tool made specifically for that type of circuit. Interchangeability and inter-operability may not be the most important features. This is a consequence of the abundance of choice which we confront repeatedly.

Indeed, the business potential of equipment for offices based on the computational machines is enormous. This is a center of complexity where the intermingling of business and technology is greatest. A study of the history of the development of calculating machines reveals a long list of ways in which business drives technology, and *vice versa*.

Let us return briefly to the case of computers as cash registers or point-of-sales machines. Recently many supermarkets have introduced computerized inventory systems. Goods are bar-coded to allow optical reading of the product and price. The cash registers are linked into mainframe computers as remote stand-alone terminals. The checkout items are optically read as they are swept past the reader. The item description and price are displayed on a screen for the customers to verify, while the price and sales data are controlled and analyzed by the computer. As the purchases proceed, the information is used to automatically generate re-order and delivery schedules, future pricing and financial operating plans for the supermarket managers. A manual entry permits the handling of items without the bar code. In some cases, a synthesized voice provides audio output in addition to, or in place of, the visual output. The computer replacement of the cash register did not take place as anticipated, but has evolved into an efficient transaction facility compatible with the larger concept of an information network.

At this point, super-computers with capabilities for several hundreds millions instructions per second are becoming available. A question can be asked about the purpose of increasing the magnitude of our signal-processing capability, both in speed and volume. There are many answers to this question but none of them are entirely satisfactory. Probably the best answer is simply that we are just looking at what we can do and where we can go, realizing that our ability to extract meaning from data via computers is pitifully small. This leads to two other topics, namely, analog computing and knowledge engineering.

Analog computers appeared first in the form of the slide rule. For a short while analog computers for mathematical problems were popular. These used the charging and discharging of capacitors and inductors as the analogs of differentiation and integration. Hydraulics were also found to be useful as analog computing tools and could even do logic. Altogether, analog computing did not fail because of its inability to be precise; it died because digital computing methods were more than adequate to solve many of our problems.

With parallel computing and an ever-increasing demand on digital signal-processing speed, it is appropriate to propose that analog computing should be resurrected for those areas where it has significant advantages. For example, the Fourier Transform can be done more simply by optical methods. Furthermore, 2-D and 3-D signal processing is more suited to an optical analog way of signal processing. This area, in fact, will be discussed in the next chapter.

Knowledge engineering is a new term used to describe efforts towards extraction of knowledge from data. Artificial intelligence and expert systems are two areas receiving significant attention, both by the computer community as well as by the public. As these terms imply, we are attempting to tame our flood of data by reducing it into a more systematic knowledge base and, thereby, facilitate our handling of the data and deriving a new understanding from it. In another direction we are resurrecting the notion that we can bridge somewhat the knowledge and understanding gap, or in other words, the physics-to-philosophy gap. This effort is in its infancy, but the work has very important business applications. The problems being tackled in this area are very human and we sense the needs acutely.

Artificial intelligence is the simulation of our activities by the computer, such as reading an article and extracting some meaning from it, or selecting an answer appropriate to a question. We often attribute these activities to our intelligence; hence, the name artificial intelligence. The computer does this by a set of logical rules based on the building-up of knowledge by association and deduction. There are a number of different business applications of artificial intelligence.

A set of simple rules can make a machine respond in a user-friendly manner. This helps to put the user at ease when confronted with a black screen of a cold, powerful computer. Some PC's, when switched on, will show a picture which says "good morning," "good day" or "good evening," depending on the time of day, and make a statement like, "Please enter 'go' if I am familiar to you; otherwise enter 'please help'." Some PC's are also capable of answering simple questions. The hardware, which enables artificial intelligence (AI) programs written in "LISP," a language designed for AI, to run efficiently and at a high speed, is already on the market.

Expert systems are computer programs designed to simulate the role of a person who routinely analyzes relatively complex data with a set of definable rules. For example, one of the first expert systems was designed to interpret seismic survey charts for oil exploration. The expert system can analyze a chart in the same way a person trained to interpret such charts would do. Since the rules are not numerous, the machine can do the task admirably. Businesses have already sprung up to market packaged expert system software and to offer their services as knowledge engineers to write "expert system" programs for clients.

Japan announced, with a great deal of fanfare, her intentions to create the knowledge-based computer, the so-called fifth generation computer. (The vacuum tube, transistor, IC and LSI-based computers are the previous four generations.) European countries and the United States responded with their own initiatives. This competition promises to be one of the most significant activities in merging technology with human behavior and it will have a profound influence on the conduct of business as we move closer and closer to being able to master our data and knowledge resources.

Chapter 6

Optoelectronics and the Information Society

A society in which the very existence of its members is intimately dependent on its ability to harness information can justifiably be called an "Information Society." How optoelectronics technology will influence this society is a rather broad subject that cannot be discussed intelligently without first defining a restricted framework. We will start by putting some specific interpretations on the semantics of the terms to be used, and prescribe some boundaries for both optoelectronics technology and for the fields and activities whose impacts are to be measured. A semi-quantitative measure of these impacts can then be presented.

The meaning of the words—data, information and knowledge—are imprecise, and a person may use them to describe different things on different occasions. An artificially constrained interpretation of the meanings of these three words will be used for this discussion. Here—data, information and knowledge—are defined as follows:

Data:	Any recorded event
Information:	Acquired data
Knowledge:	Useful data

These interpretations may be somewhat contrary to the normally accepted meanings of these words, but they are proposed here to prevent ambiguity in our discussion. These interpretations can be justified along these lines: Any activity or event taking place any-where in the world in our society can be a piece of data. If it is recorded on paper, on film, in computer memory, or in someone's head, or if it can be deduced from other recorded events, this activity can be recalled and it is a piece of data. If an activity is not recorded, it is as if it had never taken place; therefore, it is not a piece of data. A pertinent example is a chess game between two persons. The fact that the game took place one day is incidental; it only becomes a piece of data if the moves were recorded.

Data becomes information if it is of interest to an observer who makes an effort to acquire the data. The chess game could have been played by Bobby Fisher and Gerry Kasparov in the world champion-ship series, the ultimate of chess competitions, and as such, been recorded for chess aficionados. The piece of data on the match exists, but it only becomes information when someone deliberately wants it for some purpose; hence, information is acquired data. To clarify this further, consider a news broadcast. A viewer might only be looking for the World Cup results of the day. The rest of the news is totally insignificant to him. Only the World Cup result, Italy 2, Argentina 1, is information to him.

Along this same line of argument, knowledge is defined as useful data. Data are increasing exponentially in our society. Most data have very limited usefulness; much is redundant. Our data, however, are usually filtered by interested persons, and assembled into useful categories. Interpretations can be made, and deductive or inductive rules established. From its original unorganized state, the data are in useful form, ready for would-be users. Of course, our whole civilization is essentially an educational process of sharing experiences and developing knowledge. Hence, knowledge and useful data are synonymous.

Lest we lose the thread of our discussion of the impact of optoelectronics technology on our information society, it is important to connect data, information and knowledge with optoelectronics. To make this connection, we need to summarize first what optoelectronics technology is, and what impact it is making on different technological endeavors. Then, we can see that the processing of our data into knowledge and making it readily available is the major challenge we have today. Business successes and social development are dependent on the efficiency of information handling.

What is optoelectronics technology? It is the use of both electrons and photons to perform functions according to system requirements. Advances in fabrication techniques for electronic material, in analytic tools and in computational power, have opened up an area in which the electrons can be closely approximated to particles with specific energies, and the photons to coherent electromagnetic waves. This has greatly enhanced the prospect of being able to employ electrons and photons respectively and jointly to play their best roles. It is against this background that optoelectronics technology is developing into an ever-broadening and increasingly important technology base.

Vacuum-tube technology, in which free photon-excited electrons and free electron-excited photons are used for optoelectronic conversion, continues to play an important role. However, the present trend is to execute electron-photon interaction within a solid material. In principle, such an arrangement permits the creation of more robust, compact, reliable and efficient devices. At the same time, the guidance of photons along low-loss dielectric structures adds another dimension to the use of electrons and photons. It is now possible to envisage the processing and transportation of both electrons and photons, with or without conversion, to achieve desired performances. Optoelectronics technology includes light-generation, detection and guidance and the integration of these actions. There are now real prospects of achieving a number of significant advances in optoelectronic components with sub-picosecond response times. These include:

- Single-frequency light sources
- Detector sensitivity near quantum limit
- Transmission medium with practically zero loss and almost infinite bandwidth
- Electro-optic and nonlinear optical materials with large coefficients.

The benefits which can accrue from these advances are likely to be in improved cost and performance for all system products that relate to equipment for communication, control and computer applications. More specifically, the impact will be felt in information-transmission systems, storage systems, signal-processing applications and sensor technology. The impact will increasingly be felt in the network, service and general commerce areas. These aspects will now be described in some detail.

Information transmission, storage and processing have been developing somewhat independently; on the other hand, sensor development, more akin to man-machine interaction and interfaces, is considered a totally non-related area of technology. The impact of optoelectronics technology in these areas is highly significant. The performance of these systems will be improved and their use will be merged more closely.

In the long term, the implementation of information networks is likely to change radically as new system capability makes flexible broadband networks feasible and as the demand for new services replaces traditional communication activities. These new systems will in turn result in a redistribution of general commercial activities.

Currently, information-transmission systems handle mainly the transmission and distribution of telephone and data traffic. TV and video signals are distributed separately, usually in a broadcast mode. The introduction of optical-fiber transmission systems and the use of optoelectronics technology have already demonstrated significant cost reductions for the long-distance trunk connections. This technology will soon prove to be cost-effective for local area networks and subscriber-distribution applications. The near-term quest is to utilize the fiber systems along with the existing copper network. The use of old and new technologies will permit an infrastructure of fiber systems with a much larger potential capacity for carrying information to be built up gradually. Narrowband signals for voice and data may be handled in an integrated fashion in the Integrated Services Digital Network (ISDN) environment. Efforts are also under way to incorporate videophone service into a new broadband network. The evolution from a narrowband into a broadband network is, however, a complex issue involving considerations of both system costs and service provisions. An optical-fiber transmission system is essential to this development since an increase in bandwidth of nearly a thousand-fold is required. Such an increase in bandwidth cannot be handled without optical fibers. However, the service provisions and eventual network configurations are open-ended challenges. The current situation calls initially for mass-producible, low-cost, optical-to-electronic and electronic-to-optical conversion units. Optoelectronics technology is certainly progressing in the right direction.

Up to now, information storage has been associated with computer systems. Large amounts of data are stored in Random Access Memories (RAM) as well as in slower but larger storage media such as magnetic tapes and discs. With the inception of computer networking, there is an increasing need to transport stored data. Optoelectronics technology is making an impact in this area with the introduction of laser optical discs. Furthermore, optical interconnections for electronic circuits are reducing electrical interference and later signal differential-delay problems.

In the ISDN environment, machine-to-machine communication is seen as another service aspect of the network. This will make information storage a part of the communication-system requirement. High-speed, store-and-forward procedures for data will undoubtedly be demanded.

Information processing is needed for a variety of reasons. Speech and visual information must be transformed to a convenient electrical form for ease of transmission and storage. Data may have to be transformed for the same reasons. Data may even have to be manipulated in computation and coding. Speech and visual information may also have to be manipulated to extract features or to reduce redundant information. Speech and picture synthesis and recognition are examples of information-processing actions; coding and encryption are other examples. These latter two activities are needed to improve data safety. Obviously, information processing takes a great variety of forms and requires different ways of handling. However, greater signal-processing speed usually can be used advantageously.

Optoelectronics has played crucial roles in signal processing, particularly with visual/pictorial information. Photocopiers, video cameras and optical radar are a few examples of devices that use optoelectronics. Recent signal-processing activities include laser bar-code scanners, holographic interference deformation measurement and laser printing. Also, there is a great variety of applications of optical wave-front transformations to achieve Fourier transformation, correlation and convolution of signals.

A relatively minor although widespread use of optoelectronic devices is for intrusion-detection systems which sense the interruption of an optical beam. Actual alarm systems work with a collimated optical beam generated by a light-emitting diode (LED) and a collimating lens directed at a photodetector that is placed in a line of sight with the beam, but at a remote location. The interruption of the beam triggers the alarm. Elevators use such systems to initiate the closing of doors. Some escalators and automatic water-flushing systems use beam interruption as a command to start or stop.

Another sensing system which uses optoelectronic detection is light-level sensors. A photodetector is used to sense light levels for camera systems or to switch street lights on automatically. The introduction of lasers and optical fibers has catapulted optoelectronics into the sensor field in a major way. The coherent laser has been recognized as a range-and-rate sensor. Lidar (optical radar) is capable of measuring distances very accurately. The laser has even been proposed as a means of establishing standards for length and time. Furthermore, an oscillating-ring laser is a rotational-rate sensor with no moving parts that can be made with resolutions equal to, or exceeding, the resolution of mechanical gyros. The Doppler-shift effect, combined with light scattering, can also be used in flow-velocity sensors. The fiber waveguide, in conjunction with lasers and detectors, has very good feasibility as a universal sensor for physical parameters such as temperature, pressure, strain, rates, etc. Fiber waveguide sensors work by registering the change in the propagation characteristic of the fiber caused by a change in the specific physical parameter to be measured. For example, a fiber can be used as a temperature sensor if a temperature change causes a specific change in some parameter of the propagation of light through it. One way to do this is to sense the phase of a part of an optical signal traveling through a length of fiber. This phase signal is compared with that of another part of the same signal traveling through a reference fiber. The sensing fiber is exposed to the temperature change. As a result, the length of the sensing fiber changes due to thermal expansion, and the phase of the signal through that fiber is altered. An optical-detection arrangement can readily be made, for example, in the form of an interferometer, that can be used to detect the phase change. Since the phase change is dependent on fiber length, extremely high sensitivity can be achieved by the use of long lengths of low-loss fiber. The same arrangement can be used for pressure sensing. In fact, the first proposed sensor application was an acoustic pressure sensor in a sonar system. Obviously, fiber sensors are not without disadvantages. Many practical problems exist in the mechanical design and in the separation of wanted signals from unwanted signals.

Fibers in coil form have already been demonstrated as a rotational-rate sensor. Fibers can also be used as a tether to moving vehicles so that other sensing equipment carried on the vehicle can be linked to ground-based or to other moving-platform-based equipment to execute sensing and navigation. These types of application suggest that optoelectronic sensing is evolving. Not only is a broad range of improved and novel sensors available, but the signals generated by the sensors can be used conveniently as direct inputs to signal-processing and transmission equipment.

Unmistakably, the trend is towards the merging of various technologies which previously were concerned with separate application areas. In many ways this comes as no surprise. In the course of development in our society we have repeatedly reassessed separate developments into a more coherent whole. The transmission, storage and processing of information are being integrated into a single area under the impetus of providing an integrated service. If sensors are considered as another form of service, then they are a part of the same system environment. Indeed, the development of robotics will accelerate this trend. Robots are merely computer-controlled machine tools which use many sensors. As such, robots eventually must be incorporated into the information network for efficient and versatile use.

Man and machines already form an intimately and mutually dependent network. Many organizations store much of their operational data on computers. Each week, the payroll clerks instruct the computer to gather the information needed to prepare employees' pay checks. Banks cannot operate without computers to distribute daily interest or to balance clients' accounts. Without such machines many of the transactions could not be completed within the available time. Similarly, the turnaround of goods in stores and factories would be much slower. The variety of competitive goods would be much smaller, and possibly would offer much less value to the customers.

Consider the case of a cheese vendor who sells a line of gourmet cheeses. He has determined through his experiences with customers that soft French cheeses constitute a competitive product line. His variety of these cheeses attracts customers away from supermarkets whose offerings of these are very limited. His selection of some exotic cheeses, together with his knowledge of cheese, improves his customer relations. By carrying appealing accessories for cheese-eating, he can make large-margin sales through the impulse buying that is prompted by his shop's ambience. In operating his enterprise, he uses the telephone to order stock and to check deliveries. He has a personal computer to total his sales and to keep his accounts. He receives advertisements from suppliers. He monitors the promotional activities of his competitors on radio and TV and in newspapers and magazines. His information network is not integrated, nor is his use of information quantitatively assessed. He could easily be set on a downward spiral if a shrewd competitor appears on the scene who is determined to wrestle business away from him. This competitor could develop and use a more effective information network. Instead of using the PC only to keep accounts, he could use it to do better sales analysis. Programs are available for PCs that allow the competitor to minimize inventory cost, to accelerate turnover, and to plan sales campaigns. The competitor could link his PC to a network of cheese vendors and receive statistical data on popularity trends and new products. He could also link his PC to a data bank to obtain local population data. Armed with such data, the competitor could organize his sales promotions and design special programs to lure the speciality customers from other vendors by offering comparable or superior knowledge and helpfulness. The competitor may choose to branch off into wine sales rather than offer cheese accessories, since wine is also a consumable and tends not to produce a saturated market. Of course, the outcome of such a hypothetical rivalry is not certain, and return on investment is not guaranteed. However, the integrated network concept is likely to give the second merchant the competitive edge to succeed against the original vendor.

Communications networks of the world are being developed into integrated service systems because of their perceived advantages. ISDN, first started in Europe, and INS of Japan are strong efforts to establish networks that will first handle voice and data, and then extend to include a broader range of services. These additional services will eventually include broadband services based on video signals. The development of Local Area Networks (LANs) is also progressing rapidly. These LANs cater for the local needs of a group of customers. A LAN could be set up within an office complex at a geographically confined location, within a university complex, or at a single company with many geographically dispersed locations. These LANs usually interconnect computers, data stores, facsimile and telex equipment, telephones and may also provide video conferencing facilities.

Another network development is in TV distribution and multi-service broadband distribution. In the U.S., TV distribution comes in several forms. The three principal networks—NBC, CBS and ABC—and a number of local independent stations broadcast over free space and distribute their nationwide programs via satellite or trunk cables. The cable-TV companies distribute TV programs only via dedicated cables from both network stations and from a few specialized stations that broadcast just to the cable-TV distributors via satellites. These specialized stations generate only news, only sports or only movies. Cable-TV subscribers pay for the basic cable service and usually pay additional fees to receive a choice of special stations such as the movie channel. Most cable-TV distributors offer at least twenty-six channels. A third type of TV distribution provides pay-as-you-view services via the cable-TV or special satellites. This type of TV distribution network is spreading in many countries though at different rates. At the same time a number of countries have built small-scale, field-trial systems of broadband multiservice networks. Canada, Japan, the U.K., France and Germany each have one or more such experimental networks. These systems usually use fiber optics as the transmission medium and distribute one to three TV stations simultaneously, using a switching arrangement, into a subscriber's home. At the same time, the system provides FM radio reception, data and telephone channels. Videophones are supplied to some or all of the households. This type of effort is undoubtedly promoted by the recognition that a broadband distribution network to all households should increase per-capita productivity, promote expansion and redistribution of trade, and change the social structure. All of these are the expected results of improved and more effective usage of information.

Momentum for building the communications network of the future is increasing. Many ambitious nationwide and continent-wide systems are being planned. It is interesting to note that the current communications network, based on copper conductors, provides telephone services to around 1 billion households using 10 billion km of wires. Studies indicate that the per-capita GNP is directly proportional to the number of subscribers per 100 households. While it is not fair to say that the wealth of a nation can be due entirely to the quality of the communications network, it certainly seems to be true. It is also interesting to point out that a telephone requires one-thousandth of the bandwidth needed for a videophone. The future network, therefore, must handle information rates at least a thousand times larger, when the use of the videophone reaches the level of the use of today's telephone. At present, the largest bandwidth system needed for telephones is around 560 Mb/s.* This means that the bandwidth needed in the future will be in the range of 560 Gb/s.** This is a staggering information bit rate, and one that possibly can only be reached using optoelectronic techniques.

Telephone, data links, facsimile and videotext are some familiar services available for our communication needs. These services support our trading, industrial and individual activities. TV and radio are two other important services that provide entertainment and promote community links and trade through advertising. Physical transportation and printed material are also vital to our trade and industry and to individual and community needs. When broadband services can be provided over a new network, the possible types of services and their uses will undoubtedly evolve as the result of perceived benefits and competitive forces.

---

* Mb/s: megabits/sec (10^6 b/s).
** Gb/s: gigabits/sec (10^9 b/s).

Whenever information in any of its various forms helps to increase the competitive edge in business, specialized information services immediately spring up. These services provide distillation and analysis of pertinent data for special markets. Such information services are themselves subject to competitive pressure, and only the ones that do the best job of synthesizing data will survive. These services assist the growth of per-capita productivity in the manufacturing industry, and foster the profitable trading of manufactured products. Furthermore, improved information allows the consideration of factors such as the worldwide resource limits such that worldwide commerce can be expanded without generating crises.

An example will illustrate the argument just presented. Company A is large enough to set up a facility for analyzing control data and for collecting the results from these analyses and disseminating them to its units to facilitate rigorous product planning. Company B is too small to afford such a facility and yet it must compete. The choice is simple: Company B must cooperate with other companies in the same situation to have some enterprising, qualified people set up a data-analysis facility on a commercial basis to help each of them. The assumption here is that information is too vital to be ignored in the planning stage for any product that must be competitive. Therefore Company C, a service organization emerges. This process is likely to be mutually re-enforcing with the result that a hierarchy of services will be established.

Videotext is a service that has been evolving over recent years. Initially it was offered as readily accessible news in text form for TV viewers. On-demand news, timetables for various daily events, weather reports and other similar items became available to the viewers at any time. Later, more ambitious schemes such as *Presstel* in the U.K., *Bildschirmtext* in Germany, *Captain* in Japan, *Antiope* in France and *Teletext* in Canada were offered. In the U.S., legal search and financial data are offered to paying customers via special data links. So far, the penetration of these services is not widespread in the general domestic area; however, special interest groups have been well satisfied with the services that are offered. Financial institutions have found up-to-date financial data of immense benefit for improving their trading postures. Using a legal-search facility, as opposed to manual search efforts, lawyers can obtain the kinds of substantive evidence and corroborative precedents that help them win cases. When a group of travel agencies started using data on travel and vacation facilities available through a suitable travel service, both the quantity and quality of their offerings improved. The travel agencies could satisfy the individual requirements of their customers more rapidly, and could provide better matches. As a matter of fact, the fortunes of major and minor airlines are strongly dependent on their data-handling facilities. Recently, some airlines began offering computerized preboarding seat selection for any future flight. This has resulted in better control of overbooking and in a reduction in airline staff at ticket counters and in gate areas. Customer satisfaction increased and revenues started to climb.

These examples suggest strongly that information services are vital in our daily life as well as for industry and commerce. However, it is evident that service development is lagging behind technological progress. This is due in part to the inertia of our socio-economic system, but it is also due in part to the non-orderly availability of the necessary technological tools. Nevertheless, the matching of technology to information-related services is a lot closer than before.

The existence of a broadband network capable of high-quality video transmission to every home and very-high-speed data interconnections will allow the development of services not yet envisaged. The pay-as-you-view movie service offered by cable-TV operators is making substantial gains in acceptance, despite early subscriber resistance. The change came about when film distributors found that video cassettes are not popular sales items, while cassette rental is highly popular. Hence, when new technological advances allowed the cable-TV operators to offer pay-as-you-view films, the cassette renters found it more convenient just to order the film by phone rather than to make the trip to a rental place.

An ambitious scheme is under way to transform TV advertising. Advertising has traditionally been approached on an antagonistic basis. The crux of successful advertising is to catch the attention of the potential customer and lure him or her into becoming a customer. The latest scheme is to package commercials in such a way that they have entertainment value in their own right. Potential customers are then tempted to watch commercials voluntarily as part of the fun. This trend has two really significant consequences. First, advertising must be packaged differently. Initially the advertisement may be very entertaining, but eventually it probably will contain substantive discussions of values and comparisons with competitive products. Finally advertising will become interactive with the viewer. The second consequence is even more far-reaching. Successful advertising must win the potential customer's confidence and become a trusted friend. The would-be customer discovers the fact that he requires information to understand his needs and to help him determine how these needs should be satisfied. This would imply a major shift in allocation of the advertisers' resources.

Manufacturers and service providers will invest substantially in improving the information network on which their trading activity must take place. The cost per subscriber for the construction of the hardware for the broadband distribution network could be substantially higher since it can be repaid very handsomely through serving the information vendors. The investment which previously has been directed towards advertising in a purely consumable form will be directed towards the information network that will provide a data bank as well as serving consumers' needs.

"Business as usual" is still true even with the changes in the competitive environment generated by an over-abundance of product choices created by a host of available technologies. Business is still risky and uncertain but full of opportunities. The overall volume of commercial activities continues to increase. Apparently most of this increase occurs in the service section because information transmission, storage and processing facilities allow information collection, sorting, analysis and dissemination to be carried out to meet the needs of the activities. Products will have greater variety, better distribution, increased value, improved reliability, and more planned obsolescence. Most importantly, products will be lower in cost. The net result of these factors is that more wealth will be generated for more people. Of course, this statement applies at any time to describe our civilization. However, in our present era of the "information society," the emphasis is: to limit the proliferation of redundant and trivial data; to gather and distill needed data into useful forms; to broadcast data in the most informative way for users. All of these are being done in order to make better products more cheaply, and to tailor them more closely to meet specific human needs.

The environment of today is different from that of the past Industrial Age. The era of long product cycles and product differentiation by price and features is all but over. With the abundance of technology and, as a consequence, the corresponding abundance of products, "product cycle" will only be meaningful in terms of a sequence of products meeting a dynamically evolving need. Price and product differentiation become secondary to identifying needs for the target and the development the customer's perception of his need for the product. Obviously, information is the key to success. Optoelectronics, with its ability to improve information-related technology, will play an increasingly dominant role in shaping this environment.

Our excursion into a discussion of the nature of optoelectronics technology and the actions in the areas where optoelectronics technology will make an impact permits us to present a meaningful analysis of this impact.

Optoelectronics has introduced the following advantages:

- a transmission medium with nearly zero loss, infinite bandwidth and zero cost;
- an operational speed envisaged to be one thousand times the current speed of 500 Mb/s;

- an integrated-signal transmission, storage and processing system;
- sensors integrated into the information system.

The technical areas where the impact of optoelectronics will be greatest are:

- information transmission,
- information storage,
- information processing,
- sensors.

In turn, optoelectronics will penetrate into:

- the information network,
- services,
- commerce.

In this discussion the scale of this impact will be analyzed only for the technical areas.

With the prospect of single-frequency lasers and dispersion-compensated fibers operating in the 1.2 to 1.6 μm wavelength region, transmission systems based on silica fiber are expected to have steadily improving performances. The required span between repeaters will increase to several hundred kilometers. Transmitter speed will reach 10 Gb/s. Receiver sensitivity will approach 3 dB from the quantum limit. Many wavelengths, at 20 nm down to several GHz spacing, can be simultaneously carried by a single fiber in a bi-directional operating mode. For special repeaterless applications in the trans-oceanic environment, super-low-loss fibers will eventually be available. Hence, the impact in this area is to provide a means for an extremely broadband and low-cost transmission. These developments will open the way to establishing eventually a totally transparent broadband network.

The versatility of the interaction of electromagnetic waves with matter has not been explored in any depth. Even so, optical storage discs with huge capacities are already available. Holographic techniques promise to increase storage density by utilizing the volume rather than merely the surface areas of the storage medium. Integrated optical techniques for stable, portable, physically-convenient optical phase detection open the way for powerful signal processors. Even without integrated optics, optical-signal processors provide a convenient means to achieve Fourier transform, correlation and convolution. With new optically active materials such as electro-optic, photo-refractive and magneto-optic materials, sequential, parallel, and systolic signal-processing arrangements are expected. Dynamic reconfiguration is a real possibility waiting for development. Reconfiguration by holographic masks for interconnections on VLSI circuits has already been suggested. This technique will allow a new approach to solving interconnection problems, as well as offering a possibility of improving reliability and providing hardware with on-chip programming.

Since optoelectronics has the capability for high operational speeds, present approaches to signal processing are likely to be re-examined with a view to achieving a better trade-off of bandwidth versus ease of implementation and versatility. For example, in a speech-recognition system, the analysis of the signal could be extended, within the short time that it is available, so that better features can be extracted. At the same time, the same technique could be combined with a coding scheme to produce compressed speech, say at 9.6 kb/s, with better fidelity.

Optoelectronics opens the possibility of introducing a new variety of sensors for physical parameters which will not only extend versatility and sensitivity, but which also will conveniently interface with optoelectronic-signal processors, sorters and transmission systems. These sensors represent a set of key components for creating human-less factories and robots capable of working cooperatively with each other. This prediction is based on presently demonstrated sensitivities of sensors using coherent signal and fibers that are beyond those of all conventional sensors. Additionally, these sensors are inert and have remote sensing capabilities.

Do we have an abundance of information, or do we have really an abundance of data? After all the discussion of the impact of optoelectronics, we still do not have a clear answer. However, it can be deduced from the argument that we need to advance optoelectronics technology rapidly so that we can construct more powerful equipment for the transmission, storage, and processing of data. These new items of equipment are going to be very popular with users since much collation, sorting, and analysis work must be done to reduce a vast amount of data into useful information and knowledge. This information and knowledge can then be used to aid our business activities. Truly data is being generated at a near-exponential growth rate, and the interaction and cross-fertilization of the contributions of individual workers have been limited by the inherent limitations in our communication skill and facilities. For example, it is not unusual to hear someone say, "I invented this device in the U.S. and two days later another guy in Europe announced that he did the same thing"; or, "I must work hard on this concept, and I'd like to reduce it to a practice which is patentable before someone else does it." These examples illustrate the fact that we are not only communicating inefficiently, but we are also deliberately avoiding communication.

On the other hand, communication is sufficiently efficient that even in those parts of the world most remote from civilization, people are no longer surprised by aeroplanes and radios. At the same time, an idea can be extremely influential when applied at the right time. The Chinese have an ancient proverb, "A spark can start a fire which consumes the entire land," that illustrates this fact. Hence, reduction of data to information is a highly complex issue. The use of powerful machines merely helps us initially to do mechanical and rule-based analysis. We will have to struggle to find ways and means of capturing the essence of our experience and achieving flexibility in manipulating and interpreting data and of transferring the results to increasingly powerful machines.

By extending our thought processes to machines, it is conceivable that an interdependent man-machines age will come. In some minor ways it has already arrived. Without computers we are already incapable of doing many of our daily tasks such as banking, not to mention such an astonishing feat as landing on the moon. Without the car many of us could not reach our offices.

In this context, the impact of optoelectronics technology on our information society can be dimly understood.

Note: This chapter is a modified version of Chapter 25 of *Optoelectronic Technology and Lightwave Communications Systems*, edited by Chinlon Lin (N.Y.: Van Nostrand Reinhold, 1989).

Chapter 7

Development of the Information-Service Industry

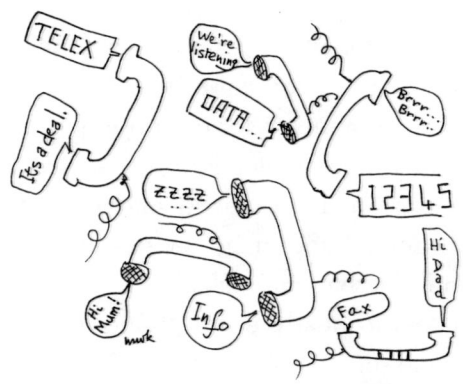

The telephone was regarded as a trivial apparatus destined to be born to blush unseen, except by the inventor and his close associates. This is a precis of an often-quoted remark made by a learned member of the professional institute after the telephone was presented at a technical session by Alexander Graham Bell. The telephone, in spite of this remark, became the basis of many profitable businesses and is an instrument essential for the development of our civilization. Without the telephone, the quality of life would certainly be much poorer. However, its role in promoting an information service industry is by no means clear. Just as its predecessors, the telegraph and the delivery of the post, the telephone is so dominant as to overshadow the continuing need to make information delivery more effective.

"At the third pip the time will be exactly 10:31. Thank you for using the dial-for-time service." Promptly, a 20-cent charge is added to your telephone bill.

"Hello, sir, I am John Wilcox. How are you this evening? If you have a minute, I would like to tell you about our Savings and Insurance Plan." A typical phone solicitation comes to a randomly chosen household.

"If you are lonely and need some excitement, please call this number: 900-666-9999. You'll find what you want." A maybe sleazy or perhaps legitimate phone service is encouraged by another phone company.

These are some of the many ways of using the telephones which have become part of the information service industry. Telephones, originally introduced as a means for person-to-person talk outside the range of direct voice communication, are an essential part of our information network. In a developed nation, there is almost one telephone per household and many phones in each business office. The national and international telephone networks allow almost instantaneous access to nearly every phone in the world from any individual telephone set. Telephone and voice contact have allowed much information to be transferred and many tasks to be performed in a smooth and timely manner. Technological advancement has continuously reduced the cost so that the service can be provided affordably to more and more people. The economic impact is understandably so dominant in this information-dominated age that many developing nations place telephone network installations high on their national priorities.

The current global network is mainly based on fixed installations of cables interconnecting every subscriber through switches and transmission cables so that specific one-to-one connections between any two users can be established. The network is the highway system for transporting the phone messages. The highway system and switches are designed to allow the interconnection of any two users without unacceptable delays and with best economy. The arrangement resembles the highway system for cars, with interchanges to allow cars to reach their destinations without having to connect each house to every other house with a special road. Now, the network is being extended to cover mobile users. A so-called cellular radio system will eventually permit all vehicles such as cars, ships and aeroplanes to have telephones while moving anywhere.

The telephone companies are service companies. Many of them offer both the telephones and the interconnecting network to their customers. The customers are often referred to as subscribers since they usually pay the telephone company a fixed fee for the rental of the telephone equipment together with a variable charge depending on the frequency, duration and distance of interconnection of their phone calls. They subscribe to the service for a fee.

The telephone service has traditionally been provided by the government or a monopolistic organization to reflect the strategic importance of such a network for a nation. Recently, free-market forces are causing a major change in the operations of telephone companies. In the U.S., the regional telephone companies are set up with a mandate to provide telephone services within the region, while the long-distance interregional connections are supplied by separate longline operators. However, the subscribers are free to connect to the network with their own equipment. The regional companies could just be network providers or they could offer other services as well. The flexibility of growth of an information network is substantially increased. These changes also coincide with a technology move towards transporting voice signals in the digital form of electrical impulses, just like those used by the telegraph system in former days, except that the transmission rate is much higher and only digits of zeros and ones are transmitted. The speech is digitized by a modulation format known as the Pulse Code Modulation (PCM) at a pulse rate of 64,000 pulses per second (or 64 kb/s). Actually speech in PCM form is indistinguishable from a stream of electrical pulses generated within a computer. A common network to carry both voice and data can be envisaged. A network capable of handling speech and data simultaneously is often referred to as ISDN, standing for Integrated Services Digital Network. Almost all telephone companies are gearing-up to make their networks ISDN compatible. The incentive is to increase the revenue base which can now be derived from both ordinary telephone speech traffic as well as from data traffic. The latter is increasing rapidly as more and more computers and other data machines must talk to each other. But what has the operation of the telephone and data machines to do with the development of the information-service industry? Of course, the usage of telephones for people to communicate and computers to process data stored in different computers is part of the information service. However, many more services are already implemented and others are envisioned. The examples given at the beginning of this and previous chapters are just a few.

Presently, the telephone for person-to-person calls is rapidly reaching saturation. Phone solicitation and campaigning really fall into the category of a relatively traditional way of using the phone. However, if we couple the phone service with data services, a new vista of further opportunities appears. We are poised to use computers and similar data-processing machines to help us to sort, list, analyze and disseminate our data as needed. Furthermore, the phone companies see this as an opportunity to extend their business base. With voice traffic only, the growth is definitely limited.

Superficially, this opportunity looks attractive, but taming our data, which is growing at an exponential rate, is a major challenge. Undoubtedly, a new information-service industry will come into existence. This will require considerable marketing innovation as well as technologically advanced equipment. However, such an industry will create real economic growth and improve our quality of life. It will transform our transportation, distribution and operational methods. It will help those companies who can adapt quickly to this new environment to grow at the expense of those who move more slowly.

The analysis of different approaches to creating information services can be very revealing. The principal problems encountered can be summed up as "Our inability to meet our information needs more efficiently and effectively than by employing human experts."

At 8:00 a.m. Tom Bauer, the engineering manager, stepped into his office. "Good morning, Jane. We have a lot to do today. Why don't we start right away? Please step into my office."

Mrs. Jane Wise is a highly competent secretary and works behind a well-equipped desk with word-processing equipment, a computer terminal and many other general-office facilities. Mrs. Wise handed Tom Bauer his agenda for the day. It showed his appointments at 9:00 a.m., 11:00 a.m., and 3:00 p.m. She also handed the signature file and his come-up file to Tom. "I am ready," said Jane. "Here are some papers for the file and let's answer these letters." Jane took dictation of half a dozen letters swiftly as Tom composed them, while referring to the incoming documents which triggered those responses. "I some-times wish that voice recognition could be better; then you would not have to waste time taking down what I said and then type it out. The whole process could be automatic. Then you, Jane, might be out of a job. No, no way will you be out of a job, but you'll be doing perhaps more interesting things!" Jane retorted, "You are not serious, Mr. Bauer? You know that you never bother to finish your letters. You always say to me: 'Put in whatever is necessary and appropriate to round the letter off.' How could you expect your voice-recognition system to supply 'whatever is necessary and appropriate'? Besides, you may get yourself into trouble over those more interesting things which you sometimes propose to me. You never know where they will lead to." They both chuckled.

"Be serious now," said her boss. "Please call Mr. A for me. I would like to see him about the news which he sent to everyone in my department without discussing it with me first. He is a good boss and has never done this type of thing to me before. Make it discreet. I do not want to upset him. After that, can you arrange for phone calls to these people on this list during the hour I have between my 9 o'clock and 11 o'clock meetings?

"Before I go to lunch, I would like to have my file on Project Tenderfoot. I would like to do a bit more homework before the afternoon meeting on that project. Incidentally, did you manage to collect all those references on Tenderfoot from the library search? The last set of references on Bigfoot which they supplied was good, but I bet that they have made a mess of this one since Tenderfoot is a code name and all we supplied for them were two lists of key words. The afternoon meeting is likely to last beyond 6:00 p.m. I'll leave the files in your safe before I leave as usual."

"The references are in your coming-up file already. I included the reference list which I got from the computer library search and, with the help of the Tenderfoot Project leader, we have identified three key papers which we managed to get copies of. They are all in the file."

"I am always grateful for such efficient service. Thank you, Jane."

"There is a telex for you and a document from the FAX machine. They need your immediate attention. They are in the coming-up file, but I would like to warn you that the FAX is from overseas and is almost illegible."

Just then the phone rang. Jane picked it up and answered. The caller was a reporter who had been pestering her to see Mr. Bauer about the alleged contamination of local streams which Mr. Bauer was still investigating. "Mr. Bauer is in conference at the moment, sir. He left instructions not to be disturbed. May I help you, please?"

We are witnessing here a typical office day of an individual manager and his secretary. Even with modern office equipment, the human roles are dominant. In fact, the role of the word-processor can be inferred as just a more powerful typewriter. The other machines do provide unique facilities, but the FAX failed to produce an acceptable output and the computer-based library search required a human expert's intervention before it was somewhat useful. Voice-activated typing is seen to have considerable limitations even though it appears to be a means at improving the work efficiency. Human skills of providing missing information or of tactfully handling outsiders are seen to be crucial in a social context.

Undoubtedly, office activities can be helped in a variety of ways by machines, but the previous discussion highlights several difficulties which can be traced to the lack of a usable database and functionally satisfactory machines. Take the telex and FAX services. These have been in existence for a number of years. The telex which transmits letters and numerals coded in 7-bit code at speeds up to 9,600 bits/s is sent along telephone lines. The text is typed with a telex typewriter, which converts the message into coded form on a tape. The tape is then read and sent by a telex machine. At the receiving end the message is decoded and converted to a typed output. This is slow and prone to human and transmission errors. It cannot be used for graphical messages since pictures cannot be converted into equilavent character codes. The FAX or facsimile equipment is designed to do for graphics what telex does for texts. The graphical message is scanned line by line and transmitted in pulse form. The message is in the form of a train of pulses which alternate between 1 and 0 for black and white picture elements called pixels. For high resolution, the size of the pixel must be suitably small and line spacings also correspondingly small. Thus, transmission speed for a page depends on resolution. The system incorporates no error correction. This usually results in picture quality degradation.

These two forms of services were welcomed by the business community even though the transmitted documents were not of the desired quality. They were good enough to get written messages through when speed was of the essence. Technology advances changed this situation rather fundamentally. The physical transport system using surface and air vehicles has been organized for overnight delivery almost anywhere in the world. The transmission system for electronic messages can handle higher transmission speeds. Telex and FAX services must undergo changes if they are to continue playing useful roles.

The options for improving telex and FAX with the use of technology are numerous. The question is whether the improved service is sufficiently attractive economically and performance-wise to be welcomed by users. An increase in speed is necessary and is easily implementable, but it may be far from sufficient. A telex message must be typed first and this is a time-consuming and labor-intensive process. However, if the original document is typed and stored as an electronically coded pulsed-signal stream, then the document can be sent simply by transmitting the coded signals. Furthermore, if a printed text can be electronically read and coded as a pulsed-signal stream, we have a solution for a printed text and its transmission electronically by telex. Taking this another step further, the coded electronic impulses can be processed in such a way as to offer editing facilities. In other words, the entire text prepared electronically in a word processor can be coupled to a high-speed telex system for transmission over long or short distances. Indeed, this is an important service with a sufficient degree of integration to be attractive. It is now known as "electronic mail."

The FAX system can similarly be improved. A high speed of transmission would allow many pixels to be handled speedily. High-resolution graphics can be transmitted. A standard A4 page of printer's quality can be transmitted in two or three seconds over an ISDN network. Even color can be incorporated. Since text is just another picture, it can be handled by the FAX system with ease. The hard copies are as good as the original and can be used with authentification as the original. Editing, however, is different and error correction is more complex.

It would appear that both systems should coexist, one for text and the other for graphics. But can text/graphics conversion be done? The answer is "yes." The conversion cost, however, is relatively high using current technologies. Basically, there is a fundamental difference between a 1-D information as in a string of words forming a text and a 2-D information as in a picture. When 2-D signal processing is better developed, the formation of a picture and a character can be totally interchangeable. When 3-D signal processing is possible, the scope for more efficient handling of information in the form of text, pictures and 3-D objects becomes most fascinating.

In the meantime, the argument for both advanced telex, which is coupled to word processing, and advanced FAX, which is coupled to picture making, stresses that they have their respective roles to play.

They address different market needs. The traditional service of speedy delivery of text and graphics has been replaced by using a remotely accessible text database which results in documents of original-like print quality. "I'll have the agreement on your desk for signature in two minutes," the lawyer said to his client 4,000 miles away. This becomes a reality with the high-speed FAX system which will be available across the world in the 1990s.

Already, newspapers and magazines are printed at distribution centers using high-resolution FAX for image transfer of the master copies. In due course, electronically delivered newspapers or books with selected hardcopy output can be made available at each household with this type of equipment. The real issue is in the cost of delivery and the cost of the provision of such devices. In the case of newspapers, the cost of service provision is supported through newspaper revenues which come from advertising. In the case of books, the cost of service is supported through book sales. Hence, electronic delivery of books is easier to implement since the revenue system is directly related to the reader. Even then, a whole infrastructure is involved in selling a book. The packaging of a book is a very important part of making a book appealing to the purchaser and accounts for much of the motivation for a person to want to own the book instead of borrowing it from the library. Therefore, electronic delivery of books must cater for these specific needs before it can be successful. The telex and FAX story unfolds rather unexpectedly. It is not surprising that telex and FAX equipment makers found a decrease in their traditional markets despite their efforts to improve their products. They must learn how the new market opportunities can be structured and exploited, particularly in view of the increasing importance of computers and data networks.

When computers were first introduced, they were just envisaged as a computational aid which could help us tackle complex calculations quickly. They were an extension of the mechanical adding machine and the slide rule. Computers are designed to have three basic parts: an input/output unit, a central arithmetic unit or a central processor (CPU) and a storage unit. A digital computer handles numbers in binary representation in the form of ON/OFF or 1 and 0 electrical pulses. The input unit accepts the data and control instructions. The CPU performs data manipulation through the use of certain logic functions such as AND, OR, etc. such that arithmetic functions of $+$, $-$, $\times$, $\div$ can be performed. The storage unit allows input/output data and intermediate values to be stored on a temporary or semi-permanent basis.

From this small beginning, computers have rapidly become a part of our daily life. Logical manipulation of data opens up a tremendous range of usages which are just beginning to be harnessed. We use computers to keep records, to compute, to control and as part of many electronic data systems.

Text and graphics in the form of electronic data can conveniently be manipulated and transported. This gives rise to the need of a network of interconnected data equipment. These items of equipment, just like human subscribers to a telephone network, can talk to each other and take concerted actions. We saw in Chapter 5 how the computer market evolved. Here the roles of the data network in the information-service industry are further illustrated and their importance emphasized. Data networks are an essential element in fostering the growth of the information-service industry.

"All ticketing agents of this office are temporarily busy. Your call is electronically held. Please hold on for a moment. Our agents will help you as soon as possible." This is a typical airline reservation service message when a caller reaches the office by phone at a busy time. The caller then hears "soothing music" for a moment or two. "Hello. I am Kay, ABC Airline. Sorry to keep you waiting. What can I do for you today?" "I would like to make a reservation for a flight from New York to Denver for next Tuesday."

Kay immediately accesses on her electronic terminal the flight data. "We have two flights to Denver from New York on that day, one at 9:30 a.m. and the other at 3:40 p.m. Is this for a one-way ticket? We have a super-saver weekday return between New York and Denver for next week." "What a pity! I just need a single. Please book me on the 9:30 a.m. flight. Can I have a pre-seat assignment?" "Sure. May I have your name, please."

As the caller gives the information, Kay enters it into her reservation computer and then reads back the record to the caller. This is a simple procedure which is made possible by the use of both humans and machines to achieve a highly complex task. First is the call-waiting facility. It involves holding the call open, temporarily connecting it to a tape recorder which is playing music continuously and then connecting it automatically as soon as a ticketing agent's line is available. This facility is provided through the private branch exchange (PBX), a telephone switch which is designed for subscriber locations with one or more incoming lines and many interconnectable users. This feature is a functional design of the PBX incorporated by the PBX makers to cater for such usages. It is pertinent to point out that a PBX maker must provide this feature if it intends to meet this market demand, which is somewhat special. It turns out that the call-waiting feature is needed for many applications and is not too costly to be incorporated in an electronic PBX. Should this not be the case, then this becomes an influential parameter in the business decision-making process. From the airline's viewpoint, this facility allows the flight-reservation service to be provided with the most efficient use of reservation personnel and with acceptable service quality. It is an example of how peak demands can be met without undue over-provision of facilities. Secondly, the agent accesses flight-schedule data on a terminal. This is relatively straightforward since the data are mostly static. Changes are made only occasionally and not continuously. Moreover, the same database serves every agent. The features needed include updatable stored data and multiple access. The organization of the data is a little bit more complex since data must be retrieved conveniently based on destination, time and/or date in order to have the relevant data to respond to specific questions. This has impact on the operating efficiency of the operator in terms of the training time needed as well as in terms of speed of response. All of this contributes to the operating cost. Third is the actual booking. This is a data update exercise. Each flight must have a file stored in the data store (often called a data bank or database). The new entry of a reservation is recorded, usually under the traveler's name, along with the details. However, for each reservation, the status of booking for that particular flight must be updated. The pre-seat assignment requires the data for each flight to include all seat assignment information. This means that the size of the data bank has to be much larger. The data update must be accessible at many locations and yet must not allow concurrent changes to be made. So far, most systems of this type rely on the statistical chance being unfavorable for two changes to be coincident.

The situation is made more complex when travel agencies can access many airline reservation systems so that they can serve their customers better by identifying the best flight in time, cost and convenience tailored to the customers' needs. The separate airline reservation system data must be simultaneously accessed and relevant data extracted by the travel agent's own system.

Most airline reservation systems have achieved more or less all the provisions stated above. Many computers are involved in this network of interconnected data banks. The question is whether the data available in this system can be used for other useful purposes for the airlines, and whether the cost can be lowered through better sharing of the resources so that the travelers can benefit. These are opportunities for the airlines, equipment makers and software houses who design the algorithms of how the system should work and produce the appropriate instructions.

In principle, an airline can use this database as a means to improve its scheduling and fare structure, and to plan new routes. The procedure, however, becomes extremely cumbersome when the database is large and the variable parameters are numerous. It puts pressure on machine computational speed and storage capacity as well as on mathematical tools and machine architecture. On the other hand, the airline reservation service—as it is currently implemented—is far superior to a totally human-operated system.

In a country with an inadequate communication network, an airline reservation must be made at the point of origin of a flight. The database of schedule and reservations status is only meaningful when kept at the flight's departure point. As a result, all travelers must make their arrangements on the spot. This can result in non-availability of seats when the demand exceeds planned capacity. The development of an airline system to meet the potential demand will be hindered by the reservation process. Even if the data can be transmitted to other centers, the process of updating by hand will rapidly clog up the process. However, even with the computer-based airline reservation systems currently in use, the human operators play a dominant role. Without the human agents the systems lack the intelligence to optimize data access. This problem is even more evident in another information service, namely the library search system.

Traditionally in a large library, the main public area is filled with an enormous file of catalog cards. No books are in sight. The reader will get the particular book by finding the catalog card and giving the details to the library assistant clerk who will then fetch the book, which is stored in one of the library bookstacks areas accessible only to the staff. If the reader is seeking some books for reference in a specific field, the task is daunting. He must go to the subject catalog and browse through stacks of cards and identify those which he wants through the abstract description or by the names of the authors known to him as appropriate. When the computer-based library search service came into being, users rejoiced at the prospect. The search for books by author is a model of efficiency. Cross-referencing subjects and authors is possible. The subject index is more finely divided to make a search somewhat simpler. Even journal articles are being catalogued. It is at this point that the library search service can make a major impact, but it is also here that this service meets its most significant set-back.

The perceived reward is so large that many institutional and private organizations continue to tackle this problem. Thousands of people are involved in making abstracts of articles. Authors are encouraged to provide a good summary and keywords to best describe the intent and purpose of their articles. Several commercially-operated search systems are offering their services to libraries and individuals. This massive effort only serves to highlight the difficulty of this task.

A first-time user is daunted by the difficulties of using this type of search system. Suppose a request is made for a search of published articles on lasers between 1965 and 1985; thousands of titles are listed. By narrowing the scope to semi-conductor lasers, a tenfold decrease of identified articles results. However, if the search is now narrowed to a set of key words such as lasers, semi-conductor lasers, InGaAsP and single-frequency operation, there may be none identified, even though probably a hundred papers related to these four key descriptions exist. The reason is simple. The search is only as good as the database. If the four key descriptions are not present on all papers which should have them, and if the search is for an exact fit, then very few papers will be identified. Furthermore, the user at one time is making a general search and at another time is looking for a particular article. The outcome can range from satisfactory to disappointing. The cost in time and effort of getting too many references can deter a user just as easily as the frustration of not getting any. The user's attitude towards computerized book and journal-article search systems soon changes.

Nevertheless, the library service is a well-established information service. The additional facilities, made possible by the data-processing machines including the computer, are increasing the role libraries can play. Libraries have the potential to be one of the main resources for all types of information services.

The specific successful example, cited before, is the search for past law cases in which judgments have a bearing on the specific case in question. This is a straightforward application of a certain special database on legal matters. The important point to be noted is not the elegance of the solution or the lack of it, but the fact that it offers advantages to the users with speed and efficiency exceeding that which can be provided by alternative means. Indeed, the information-service industry must help improve productivity of goods, concrete or ephemeral, which contribute directly to raising the quality of life.

"A picture is better than a thousand words," so a video sensation must be worth even more. The addition of full motion video to our range of capabilities must cause at least a minor revolution. Indeed, video has invaded our life since the invention of the TV and is present in a large number of households even in the poorest countries. The messages which can be conveyed, and the entertainment value it can give to the viewers are only limited by our imaginations. The provision of video as part of the information service, however, is in its infancy.

So far, TV is used almost exclusively for entertainment. News broadcasts, political debates and educational programs serve both as serious communication organs as well as providing a different form of entertainment from music, dancing, plays, etc. TV as a part of the information-service industry is very minor indeed. The U.K. introduced *Presstel* which merely uses the TV as a means for distributing graphic and text information. Germany has an equivalent system called *Bildschirmtext*. The data rate is compatible with telephone messages. The screen is used as a convenient display medium.

With the introduction of video recorders (VCR) and high-definition TV (HDTV), the building-up of a broadband transmission-network video signal is increasingly regarded as a more powerful means for communication in the future. It is also recognized that full motion pictures will permit our visual senses to be fully involved and, thereby, enable us to interact better with our machines.

Mr. Chan is an independent architect working in an office which is just a wing of his house. A client drove up to his door on a sunny morning to discuss the remodeling of his house. Some preparation work had already been carried out by Mr. Chan, who had paid a visit to the site and made a video recording of the area to be modified.

"What a lovely morning! I must say, it is nice to be able to work at home." The client greeted Mr. Chan as he entered Mr. Chan's office. "I suppose, you can relax in your flower garden when you feel like it, even in the middle of your working day."

"Well, I suppose I can these days. I seem to be able to do my work so much more quickly with all my computer-aided design (CAD) tools. I am taking on more than twice as much as I used to, but I spend only one-quarter of the time on each. I must thank my information-service friends.

"Please take a seat and let me show you what I have done." Mr. Chan motioned the client to a seat in front of a big screen. He pressed a few buttons on his hand-held remote control. The window darkened and the screen, which was a flat display, flickered to life.

The client leaned forward in his chair. "That's my house. Look at the corner, it is a mess. I am sure you understand why I want to renovate that part. The other parts are just to my liking. Was that the video you took the other day?" "Yes it was. You'll notice in a moment the outline where I propose to do remodeling. As you instructed me, you would like to make it stand out as different from the rest of the house, but yet in harmony with it. You want to capture the solar energy with this structure and reduce your total heating bill for the whole house. Finally, you want this area to be a study room where you can work quietly and overlook some aspects of your house." A red line started to trace the area to be modified and then a yellow line sketched out the outline of the new structure. "This is just to give you an overall view. The rest of the pictures are architect's drawings of the various sides of this structure. We'll run through them and then you'll be able to give me suggestions for further modifications."

Mr. Chan guided the client through his design which ended with a full 3-D view of the house with the new structure super-imposed. To the client's surprise the picture on the screen started to change again. This time one wall of the room was removed at a time and the house was rotated so that the client could see the room, as it were, through each of the four walls. "That is absolutely amazing. This modern technology is fascinating, but beyond me." the client said. "I like everything I saw except I wonder how the color scheme will look during the day and at night."

"We can simulate that for you." Promptly the same through-the-wall view was repeated, this time with the colors changing as daylight faded and the lights were switched on. "You see that these CAD tools are fantastic. We architects used to rely on our experience and our sense for good color combinations. Now we still do that, but we can verify our instincts with an instantaneous demonstration. Let me show you what would happen if you were to choose a wrong color or use inadequate lighting. See how disastrous it would be."

The client murmured an agreement. Mr. Chan gently brought the client's attention back and said, "Here is my estimated cost, $25,000 for materials and my fees. The fee is $15,000 dollars. I can recommend some builders for you." "But you only worked on it for three days. $5,000 a day is rather steep, isn't it?" "Well, no. If I had to do all this by hand, it would have taken me at least two weeks, but the CAD tools allowed me to complete the job in three days. However, I have to pay for the use of all these tools. They are expensive, but worth it.

"Let me explain these CAD tools to you. I pay for the usage time, and there is a connection fee paid to the communication network company for using the broadband network. Then, there is a charge for the actual usage time of the tools. For example, the demonstration you saw is recorded already, but if you would like to see some modifications, we have to use the tools and hence it will increase the cost.

"Basically, the first tool I use is to digitize my video picture of your house. My camera supplies range and angle information which is sufficient for the exact dimensions to be computed and stored. Then I use several tools. One is to allow a rough model to be generated with broad specifications such as: light value, permitted wall-to-window-area ratio and structural shape. This tool will allow me to adjust the design aesthetically while it takes care of structural details. Next, I specify thermal insulation requirements and special structural points. The tool converts the rough model to a prototype model. Then I use a database of materials and costs and compatibility to make some finer adjustments. The final model is nearly done.

"The viewing tool comes into play next, to allow me to test out the aesthetic value within the room and look at lighting effects. Finally a complete material list and a set of construction drawings are prepared.

"For these tools to work in real time the network must transfer large amounts of data quickly. Furthermore, I can, if clients want it, demonstrate dynamic properties. For example, the wind loading on a chimney or a bridge.

"The only worry I have is that if the network fails, I cannot access these tools for several days. I am not worried about lack of creativity. In fact, the tools help me try out new ideas. The tools are dumb without clever users. The other thing that bothers me is the lack of a really good database. My work is as good as the tools. If the tools can improve with usage—i.e. if every time the tool is used, it takes the demands made by the user into account and tries to improve upon its own performance then the tool will have a better database each time it is used."

This scenario at the architect's office is futuristic. But the CAD tools and their availability through a broadband communication system are almost within the state-of-the-art of our technology. The economic viability of a CAD tool-service provider, however, has only been partially tested, and we are not yet certain of the viability of the business of the architect who relies heavily on such a service for carrying out his work. The opportunity is definitely there. The problem is how to start the process.

These types of services can truly be regarded as part of the information-service industry since a database of materials and suppliers, along with design compatibility, must all be available CAD tool services for as many other professions as are needed. In many ways these types of services could grow to become a dominant way of advertising and distributing products.

The database requirement for the CAD tools in the above example is substantial. In particular, a list of construction materials, with performance specifications, descriptions of size, shape and color, price and delivery, is needed. To the architect this list represents the material resources available for his use.

The list must have all the elements necessary for the construction of many different designs of houses and other structures. It must provide sufficient choice so that the design is not limited unduly by the lack of suitable materials. Such a database is difficult to construct and it must be maintained so that all information is current and valid. A range of such databases is likely to be needed to meet efficiently the tailored requirements of different groups of architects in different regions. Each will have a pared-down list of materials and suppliers. Hence, the providers of such databases are acting as a supermarket for construction materials.

An astute supermarket operator will attempt to provide as many of the best goods as the customer calls for, at the best value for his customers, while keeping his operational costs at a minimum. At the same time, the manufacturers of the building material must secure the equivalent of shelf space in the database. They must also alert the intended customer to the existence and the merits of their product. In other words, they must advertise. In a database environment catchy advertisements must be backed up by solid product differentiation. Manufacturers A and B may make an identical product at an identical cost. Manufacturer A could have a price advantage in region A where it is located and where it has an efficient distribution system. In that case the product from manufacturer A would be listed in the database for region A. Manufacturer B should not attempt to seek a listing in the same database. It is apparent that the usual business activities continue, but the techniques used in advertising and selling could be significantly different. The manufacturers must target their products precisely for an intended customer base and then organize the listing of their product in a database such that their product provides the function which satisfies a niche market at an affordable and competitive price. The advertising is now designed as an offer of help, by defining precisely the intent of the product for the intended customers, rather than as a means of attracting attention by forcing customers to take note. The cold database environment is not amenable to hot advertising. The current abundance of choice of a large number of products with small differentiation has been created by our technological progress. Under this situation customers who want to seek the best fit for their requirements are confused by too much choice. The electronic database offers a way to meet requirements more precisely and to simplify the problem of choice. It is an appropriate solution. The demand for such services is definitely on the increase. This will raise our quality of life since our wishes can be met more precisely that way. The provision of such services will involve a large sector of our information-dominated society, gradually supplementing even the retail outlets. It will change our way of making and distributing goods, as well as our advertising and selling.

Just like all social changes, the creation of an information-service industry will be gradual and almost imperceptible. The identification of useful databases which can be implemented with existing equipment will come first. These will be explored as business opportunities; this is already happening. These new databases are likely to be the next wave of business opportunities for manufacturers of equipment as well as service providers and users because each of these groups will derive benefits in revenue generation and/or in increased competitiveness. Through the experience gained, the databases will be improved and made less static; some will even become living databases. When supplemented with new equipment made possible through the application of technology, the usage of databases will expand broadly and synergistically into every aspect of our daily life. The information-service industry will have matured.

Chapter 8

The Changing Roles of Research, Development and Production

What made the roles of research, development and production change is the richness of interplay between technology and business in our age of unlimited opportunities. Our ability to tailor products and services nearer to personal choices has raised the level of sophistication of our individual tastes and of our expectations. At the same time, our technologies are by no means complete or suitably developed and ready to help us to achieve our specific goals. The need for research and development is escalating. Competitive pressure between products has increased significantly. New products with markedly different features can rapidly make related products obsolete. Product cycles appear to be short and unpredictable. Within such an environment, the approach to research, development and production must be revised through a better understanding of these underlying developments. Otherwise, the resources needed and the effectiveness of these investments are likely to be out of line with requirements for successful businesses.

Our tastes and expectations are the basis of business opportunities. Our knowledge and our experience with technology are the tools helping us to dream up and realize products to meet these opportunities. Relevant data must be gathered and disseminated. Until the ultimate information service comes into existence, our individual ability to gather and disseminate data is strictly limited. We must utilize our own database effectively to help us target our business opportunities. Research and development are needed to enable our technological database to be augmented with new data. They must be carefully matched to our business needs since the resources available to conduct R&D are usually scarce and expensive. Furthermore, recent technological progress is making the technology base wider, more interrelated, more pervasive, and more influential. This new data gap in the technological base of companies is difficult to bridge and, at the same time, could seriously impact the ability of a company to do business. Thus it is a challenge which must be adequately met. The appropriate solution for each enterprise is influenced by the company's background and its business requirements, as well as its available financial and human resources. In general, the following are needed:

- Broad appreciation of technology's current status and trend.
- Thorough assessment of the complete technology needs of a product during its entire planned product cycle.
- Sharing of resources with R&D partners to ease the cost burden.
- Joint mobilization of efforts to introduce new technology to the public in order to gain broad acceptance and credibility.
- New technology regarded not as a right to create a new product but rather as a force to enable certain new products to come into existence.

A few practical examples can make these points clearer.

Opa Incorporated is a well-established company which has been making windows for over fifty years. It is situated in a conservative city of around 200,000 people in the sunbelt, where winters are mild but summers are long and warm. It produces around 50,000 windows per year with an average selling price of $100 per window. It supplies windows to the builders of new homes as well as to renovators of old homes. The basic style is designed for colonial-style houses with partitioning within the window frame. Technology innovation had already wreaked havoc when composite wood moldings were introduced and became a fashion. The management of the company reacted late, but not too late to keep its products price competitive. Streamlined assembly techniques were also adopted. Recently, several technological developments began changing the business base of this type of manufacturer.

1. Public awareness of the high cost of heating and cooling of a house, and the central role windows play in keeping down the running cost of a house.
2. Standard size windows are increasingly being fitted into new houses.
3. Better material and design of window structures can provide good thermal insulation and acoustic isolation.
4. Renovation activity is towards using standardized windows produced with improved technologies.

Once again, Opa Inc. is in trouble. Its small revenue of five million dollars a year cannot support a great deal of internal development effort. The cost of having an engineering activity can easily exceed 2% of revenue. In the competitive area of housing industries, 2% engineering cost is an industrial average. Yet Opa's products must be upgraded. Usually, in this situation, a somewhat experienced design engineer is hired and is told to improve the product. However, the effort is rarely optimum. The improved product is likely to incorporate only new features well known at the time. For example, it may have vacuum-sealed double glazing and polyurethane foamed strips for weather sealing. The whole factory is reorganized to cater for the new assembly tools and procedures. The new size standards will be adopted.

What is unlikely to be done simultaneously is to anticipate future requirements, marketing environment changes and the new competitive postures. Opa, in modernizing its product, has moved from a niche market into a commodity market. Both marketing strategies and competitive posture have changed. In addition to being also-runs, its products have not been optimized through choices of materials and assembly techniques to have the lowest cost with maximum value. For example, a vacuum-sealed double-glazed unit offers excellent thermal and acoustic isolation, but is a high cost assembly requiring expensive machines and the use of expensive material and a skillful labor force for operation and maintenance. An unsealed unit gives condensation problems, as well as less acoustic isolation. The wisdom of choice depends on the business target and the technological knowledge.

Technological progress is posing threats to old-fashioned small businesses. Opa Inc. may survive for a while since it has a well-established customer base. But it is struggling precariously. The sad fact is that almost no one is ready to provide effective help for this company. It must be changed into a new entity to serve a new market niche. What is needed are technical service organizations to map out for Opa Inc. the real choices based on the awareness of the status and trends of the technological impacts on research, development and production of this class of products in the building industry and housing businesses.

Opa Inc. is one of many small businesses across many different industries and business sectors. They all face the same problem, namely, increased competition from attractive new products which technological advancement has brought into existence and which threaten to wipe their established products out of existence. The solutions needed are often unique and must be tailored to each particular company even though the underlying principles are the same.

Xany is a high-technology company attempting to compete in the NMR Tomography area. It is a venture-capital funded company and is headed by Dr. Xan who has a doctorate in physics in NMR spectroscopy. His co-founders cover mechanical engineering, marketing and law. NMR Tomography employs nuclear magnetic resonance (NMR) effects to identify different constituent materials within the human body. It is non-invasive in contrast to X-ray, and offers a means to map the body just as X-rays do. Tomography is a means to detect scattered signals from the body in such a way that the signals from various detectors, strategically placed in a region surrounding a body, can be analyzed by computers to form cross-sectional maps of the body. This technique has made exploratory surgery obsolete since it can provide a three-dimensional view of the body, including the inside of the body, without subjecting the patient to physical trauma or damage in any way.

Dr. Xan is confident of success since he managed to assemble a complementary team of experts. He once said at a publicity function organized by his marketing partner for the administrators of a large number of private and public hospitals: "Our company recognizes the two major problems of NMR Tomography or MRI (Magnetic Resonance Imaging). One is that it costs too much for a small hospital to afford, and two is that the large manufacturers are in no position to reduce the cost. I have a great team here who can deliver a machine to you in one year. All of you can afford at least one, if not one in each of your departments. We can make such a promise because we are a small team with a relevant and complete database which will enable us to build such a machine without expending further resources to acquire needed information through R&D. Our job is to engineer this product and deliver it to you to meet your needs in quality, quantity, time and at a bargain price. We know exactly what you want, and we have tailored the machine to your specific requirements. Some of you, in due course, will want more features, but this is for the future. We'll work with you to add these new features as time goes along, but you will be content to have your hand on your own NMR Tomography machine with all the important features such as full resolution scan, zoom and exploratory scan.

"Please look at the model on our demonstration computer. The machine consists of a scanning chamber with detachable detectors. A sliding platform is driven with mechanisms outside the chamber in order to minimize interference signals which would have to be removed through signal processing. This feature is just good engineering since it does not change engineering cost appreciably. We can fit to our machine any magnet made by any NMR Tomography maker but will recommend our simple design which provides a uniform field sufficient for our needs. We employ a calibration scheme to take into consideration signal distortion due to a certain amount of field non-uniformity. Our signal-processing scheme is hardware/software dependent. We have a version which provides full resolution scanning and zoom through hardware. Therefore it increases image quality, has fast processing time and low-cost signal processing. Other features are obviously possible. Please note that the computer-aided design means good modularity and excellent form, fit and function of parts.

"I hope you are suitably impressed with this computer demonstration. But let me point out some other benefits. An obvious one is the fact that the computer is a design tool as well as a demonstration unit. If one of you should see a potential problem, we can demonstrate if the problem is real and we could do our design modification immediately. I should add that this terminal is directly linked with our control computer complex. In addition, our hardware is coupled with our software so that modifications can be cross-referenced and checked for interactive effects. This simplifies both software and hardware development. The basic software for signal feature extraction and display is borrowed, or lifted under license, from the Tomography patent holder."

"How much does the machine cost?" said someone in the audience. To everyone's surprise Dr. Xan said, "We want to sell it to you at as low a price as we can, so I would like to take orders first before giving you a price. For your safeguard, we will state that the order is void if our price exceeds your expectations. I would like to give you a price of 30% of a current X-ray tomography as a guideline."

Some twenty hands went up to indicate the number of probable orders from this audience of fifty people. The marketing director had carefully chosen these people from the purse-holding community of targeted hospitals. The statistical implications of these twenty orders would allow him to get a good fix on the number of machines which will be made and delivered in his first batch production. He was pleased with the numbers. His confidence in achieving the sales goal was raised. This, he mused, is indeed the old-fashioned management by objective, except that it is more like self-fulfilling prophecy. In other words, a choice fulfilled.

"We target our customers and then design, develop and produce what they want with our background and foreground research, development and production resources. Our next target can be set higher when the time comes."

The impact of research, development and production can be clearly seen to be dominant in this story about Xany. But does it mean that Dr. Xan and his co-founders have undersold their talent and background expertise? Who paid their salaries when they were building up their knowledge? Does it mean that large companies have invested in R&D only to foster future competition? Can large companies recover their R&D costs and still be competitive? How should government promote R&D activities in universities, at government R&D institutes and in industry? Is R&D the real stimulant for product innovation or are our perceived needs the driving force? Or is it the interaction of both? We shall address these questions further in the next chapter. It is sufficient here to say that R&D and production play a dominant role in the creation of this NMR Tomography business. Xany is a typical example of how R&D results can be turned into a product which meets a real need. Leaving aside the business aspects for the moment, the process of R&D should be clarified further.

Dr. Xan and his colleagues did a lot of work prior to coming together to form this venture. Each has built up significant experiences in his respective expertise. During those periods we can assume that they contributed satisfactorily or even outstandingly to their employers. In other words, they are unlikely to be parasites of some larger organizations. Now they are brought together by the common interest of establishing a new business. There is nothing sinister or extraordinary in this evolution. In fact, they could come together within a larger corporation rather than being funded by venture capital. The R&D and production experiences of these individuals are there to be exploited.

It is easy to conclude that the formation of a pool of relevant talent tailored to the task is an important and necessary condition. If suitable core talents are present, the task can be tackled efficiently. However, it is most unlikely that the core talents can cover every technical aspect needed to perform the task. More likely, it is almost certain that a great deal of reliance must be placed on other experts.

In his effort to produce the NMR Tomograph, Dr. Xan assembled a core team. They have solid expertise and experience, but they are not likely to have many of the tools and support to actually produce the equipment. They must assemble some in-house capability and obtain other facilities from suppliers. Even their technical background is probably far from complete. They need to consult with other experts and to work with a network of people. A complete infrastructure must be present.

Dr. Xan is a NMR expert. He has his university contacts for obtaining theoretical and basic knowledge. For example, the lack of contrast of two different body tissues is a well-known problem to him, but the interaction of drug-induced contrast is a new area of research. He needs such information to help him in making a technical design choice for his equipment. It would be very expensive and time-consuming to repeat this experiment in-house. He can simply make the necessary contact with his friends. Sometimes he can persuade them to do extra experiments specially to verify a point or confirm the results of some preliminary work. The sharing of resources in this way is possible and desirable. It helps everyone. The other experts may like to know the answers to these particular questions once their attention is alerted or they may like to have additional funds to augment their research resources. It is an interdependent situation.

Dr. Xan's signal-processing equipment is made by two outside companies. One supplies the basic computer and the other the basic software. His data-processing expert makes sure that the software can be adapted to run on the tomograph with supplementary software and hardware to match the computer, the existing software and the special requirements of the tomograph. Of course, the selection of these parts and their adaptation are challenging tasks which are highly dependent on the background knowledge of Dr. Xan's data expert. Sometimes the situation may justify an in-house development of both the software and hardware from scratch. However, a requirement for extensive development usually indicates that the product is probably premature and should be postponed.

For diagnostic interpretation, Dr. Xan seriously considered introducing a special feature to his tomograph. He held a meeting with his colleagues to discuss whether "expert system" technology should be incorporated to add pizzaz and attractive user-friendly features.

"I hear that artificial-intelligence people have been developing diagnostic aids such as 'MYCIN.' Do we know whether we can buy an off-the-shelf program designed to interpret tomograph results? If not, can we consider getting an outstanding company to undertake such a task?" Dr. Xan asked.

His data-processing expert, whose experience had really been in pattern recognition, volunteered: "I am not up in that area, but I am willing to look into it. Perhaps my pattern recognition algorithm can be put into 'expert system' form easily."

A second computer expert, Dr. Prom, on Dr. Xan's staff commented: "I rejected that idea since 'expert system' is in its early stages of development. While it has been successful for certain applications, each of the programs takes a long time to develop and they only provide rather limited functionalities."

Dr. Xan: "Perhaps I should explain my idea. I would like to add just a hint of a future feature to our product. At this moment, I will be happy if the 'expert system' function can only answer such questions as 'Is this a good film' or flash a warning: 'malfunction of detector R14; please adjust and rescan.' I think it is important to consider how an expert system can be incorporated so that we can design our machine to have that as a future option. We need to stretch our minds in all directions. I agree with Dr. Prom that the time is not right to incorporate 'expert system' features seriously, but I have a hunch that a demonstration of our forward thinking will help push our marketing advantages."

Prom responded rapidly: "Our resources are already stretched thinly. We cannot afford to waste time on that."

Mr. Constantin, from the production area, who had extensive computer-aided production experience interjected: "Surely the question we should address is how the provision of this feature will affect our total system design. I assume that what we are aiming for, as Dr. Xan has convinced us in our strategy meeting, is a two-cycle product. We make the first batch of one design during the first year and then make a second batch in three years with some added features and lowered cost through increased volume of sales and from our first production experience. Under this scenario the expert system enhancement is relevant. If we can incorporate this feature with no significant impact on our system design, or if we can make a little change to our system architecture so that the incorporation of this feature is possible, then we should do it. Marketing guys will pat us on our backs for making their job easier."

Dr. Xan's marketing expert was quick to take this up. "We have sufficient advantages and we have targeted our customers exactly. Meeting our delivery dates is the most important issue. For our second round I believe we could win through our price. The additional attractive feature is a luxury. Since Dr. Xan brings this up, I believe I would certainly like the system design people to consider the implication of introducing 'expert system' with the help of some outside expert system developer. We have some internal knowledge for this exercise to be carried out meaningfully."

It is to be noted that appreciation of technology must ideally be in significant depth and resident internally in the team engaged in the project. The implementation usually cannot be handled economically by the internal project team alone. In a small venture capital company such as Dr. Xan's, the choice must be to seek external help. In a large organization, a resident group working on "enabling technologies" may be justified, if these "enabling technologies" can be applied to a large number of projects under development.

The key issues brought out in this discussion on the roles of research, development and production in small high-technology companies or project teams, are the need to have an overall appreciation of the value of technology, an in-depth understanding of the key technologies applicable to the project, and a willingness to rely on an infrastructure which can supply the relevant technological knowledge or tools for the project to be totally completed. The last key issue requires an assessment of the resources in both talent and time to cover any needed missing technology gaps.

It is also clear that those key issues are applicable in both large companies with ample resources and in small, highly focused companies born from entrepreneurship. In fact, the role of research, development and production in a large company can be similar to that of consultants providing services.

Everything Inc. is a big conglomerate engaged in many businesses including automotive parts, telecommunications equipment and computers. Their technical facilities include one central R&D lab and a host of engineering centers at various manufacturing units. The technical director, Dr. Omni, is given the task by the CEO of organizing central R&D activities to meet the new business environment.

At a special briefing to the CEO and the top management team, Dr. Omni states: "The roles of research, development and production are strongly and permanently altered by recent technological advances. I was very happy when you instructed me to formulate new central R&D activities in response to this new technical environment. Today, after one year of preparation, I would like to report to you my recommended actions as well as to present to you the organization of our central R&D laboratory both in structure and in R&D activities. This is made possible through generous and selfless support from the general management of all units and from yourselves, given to me and my staff during this preparatory period.

"Chart 1 is the mission statement."

- The Central R&D Laboratory undertakes research and advanced development activities which will support unit business activities by providing broadly useful tools, enabling technologies to improve current businesses and selective technology thrusts as a basis for developing related new businesses.

"This statement has an implied precision of targeting as compared with our previous mission statement. This need for targeting more precisely and narrowly will become obvious later.

"Chart 2 is the description of the new technological environment."

- Basic research areas are becoming more interdisciplinary.

"In other words, development in a given basic area will be accelerated by progress in physics, chemistry and mathematics in an inter-linked fashion."

- The research forefront is limited by tools and instruments.

"The tools and instruments for basic research are sophisticated and complex and, hence, very expensive. They require specialists to operate them. The successful development of new electronic devices and materials requires the use of these new tools for acquiring new understanding before significant progress can be made. Hence, research costs, in terms of both money and people, are escalating. This leads to a need to share resources wherever feasible."

- A large variety of new things can be made and new activities can be begun.

"The proliferation of what can be done, derived from recent technological achievements, is rapid and unbounded. This offers unlimited opportunities but raises management issues of what would be best to meet the company's business objectives."

• Almost any project will require a breadth of new technologies.

"This is a corollary of the new technology environment. It emphasizes that we should plan our 'mix' of in-house activities and purchases of outside assistance as best fits our resources."

• Technology and the market interact strongly.

"Accordingly, I have introduced many actions during this interim phase. Almost at the very beginning, a number of our senior scientists and technologists were asked to review and initiate programs designed to gain some first-hand understanding of a number of technological areas which, in their opinion, are emerging and are of the highest relevance to us. Simultaneously, the users of technologies at our units' engineering departments were enlisted into groups, each of which addresses a key technology area. Much relevant data has been gathered through this process. Within the last three months, efforts were made to compile these data into action proposals by a small group working with me. Today we can present to you our conclusions and some recommended actions.

"Chart 3 summarizes the conclusions."

• A long-range research program is needed to set the future trend of technology which will yield results of broad significance.
• Several programs are needed in the "enabling technologies" most appropriate for our current and anticipated products.
• A few speculative programs form the basis for possible new businesses.
• A natural flow and connectivity should exist between these programs in order to facilitate technology transfer and provide synergism and a sharing of resources.

- A greater reliance is to be placed on outside help on both cooperative and contract bases.

"Chart 4 provides a list of recommendations."

- We are to adopt a strategy which will give us leadership in our chosen product lines.
- We must undertake our marketing and our product development activities simultaneously and in an integrative manner.
- The Central R&D Laboratory should still have the three traditional components:
  (a) A nucleus of stable projects in those areas which support our strategy of leadership in our chosen product lines.
  (b) The management of outside contract projects in the same areas.
  (c) Short-term projects for solving current problems.

"Accordingly the lab structure can be a matrix organization."

	Long-term research ($I = 2, E = 1$)	Enabling technologies ($I = 6, E = 9$)	Action teams ($I = 2$)
Basic programs	80%	20%	5%
Speculative programs	15%	40%	5%
Service to HQ and units	5%	40%	90%

  I = Internal lab
  E = External units + outside
  Total funding sources (I and E): 20

"It is workable to have a technical and an administrative director at equal levels of authority overseeing the technical excellence and administrative effectiveness. Three heads, respectively, look after the long-term research, the enabling technologies and the action teams, while members of their staff can be appointed to assume program, project and service responsibilities. The matrix format assures interaction and technology flow. Funding sources are from a steady internal lab fund of 50% of the total and a variable external fund, including possibly direct funding from the units, of 10%–20% and external funding of 40%–30%. The application of funding is to be about 70% for internal work and 30% for funding work contracted to the outside. Of course, the actual percentages will change with time and with our business strategy.

"The conclusions given mean that our current projects will gradually be phased to meet the new requirements. I am happy to report that the natural evolution which has been going on over the last few years has left us with a re-organization process which will not be highly disruptive. A legacy of the past operation is the proliferation of relatively small projects resulting from a lack of targeting and focusing. Another legacy is the work on a range of speculative research projects below the critical mass and without a reasonable chance of developing into viable businesses at an affordable expenditure of our resources, given our business targets and resources. These will be drastically curtailed, since a well-designed long-range project compatible with our strategic business plan will capture much of the essence of these speculation projects. Projects related to the enabling technologies are already on-going since the recognition of the importance of these enabling technologies has been realized over the past years. The new grouping increases the size of each unit to critical mass and allows a better response to the requirements of our operating units. Some of those projects are likely to attract funding from external customers whose interests are similar to ours. It is useful to point out that with the current proliferation of technology, it is important to have a broad circle of people working in unison. The combined voice can speak more convincingly and with a greater sense of credibility. Furthermore, the larger number of opinions will help the researchers avoid self-deceptive paths.

"If you will permit, I shall break here for some questions before presenting the rationale for the choice of our long-range research project."

"Congratulations. So far, I feel comfortable. Perhaps my colleagues would like to ask Dr. Omni some questions," responded the CEO.

Mr. Knightingale, the comptroller, said, "Can you still operate with our current way of deriving our R&D resources and redistributing them to the Central R&D Laboratory and the engineering centers?"

"This is a delicate issue. I am asking for a larger say in what projects the Central Laboratory should undertake, but I am not asking for a higher percentage of R&D funds to go to the Central Laboratory. I can live with our existing way of deriving our R&D funding. However, I believe that with the new scheme of accountability, the role and missions of the engineering centers of our units should be looked at carefully. In principle, the units should see that their engineering activities are more targeted. Furthermore, based on the better forecasts and expectations provided by the Central Laboratory, managers of the engineering centers can rely more on the Central Lab for future guidance and they can reduce their own less significant and speculative, or sometimes unsound, technical investments."

"I am an operations man and I always like to keep the check-and-balance position of different headquarters functions clear," Mr. Stone, the operations director, barked. "Your implied message is that with your gee-wiz lab people, you can see the future more clearly. Are you saying that your words should be taken as gospel?"

Omni smiled broadly and bowed humbly, "By all means, that's what I am saying. But please note, my people can only do a credible job if we receive clearly mapped-out business targets from top management. In fact, my dear Mr. Stone, we are going to urge you to check our projected income statements and balance sheets from an operations viewpoint to make certain that our assumptions of capital outlays and other cash outflows and inflows are in line. We often fall into a technology-driven trap which calls for large capital investment. This means that the total volume of business required to recover our costs and still make a reasonable profit exceeds that which we can expect from our targeted customer base. In other words, the required sales volume cannot be achieved with our marketing resources, given the size of the market and a realistic market share."

The manufacturing director expressed his dismay at not seeing explicit technology to help solve his manufacturing problems. Dr. Omni responded by saying that enabling technology does include production technology, for example, the VLSI and its impact on the electronics equipment assembly. He agreed that the manufacturing issue was sufficiently important to warrant the creation of an entirely new central activity to address it.

Mr. Pick, the legal director, questioned the wisdom of sharing R&D results and asked, "Shall we stop filing more patents since we cannot defend them?" Dr. Omni was alarmed by this attack. He had not considered how the sharing of information, which is needed to broaden support, impacts on patent rights. He asked for a meeting with Mr. Pick to work out patent filing and information disclosure procedures. Omni said, "This is a critical issue of our time. We must have both the patent right and the disclosure right."

The CEO was visibly pleased with the proceedings, "I have no questions at this stage. Please proceed."

Omni circulated a prepared document entitled, "A View from Industry of the 10^{12} b/s Optoelectronics Project." "This is the starting point of our new longer-term research activity."

A View from Industry of the 10^{12} b/s Optoelectronics Project

A large corporation, engaged in a range of high-technology business, utilizes a very broad range of interrelated scientific and technological knowledge. Typically focused R&D programs for perceived needs in near and longer terms are in progress. The effectiveness of these programs becomes increasingly more difficult to assure, particularly for the longer-term efforts, as scientific and technological progress proliferates. The difficulties are not only in making the proper choice, but also in containing the size of investment while ensuring effectiveness. The solution is to have two basic, but directed, research programs, one viewed from the material/device standpoint towards systems, the other viewed from the system standpoint towards circuits and functionalities. A well-chosen challenging goal should generate the proper focus to address major issues and to develop a proper perspective of technology trends. These can be utilized as trend setters, links to the broad scientific community, as the means to assess future relevance of other R&D programs and as the generator of important relevant future-assured new R&D programs for nearer-term applications.

The optoelectronics technology project is the material/device-based program. The goal is to achieve possibly 10^{12} b/s signal-processing speed by using optoelectronics technology. The impact will extend to all system products, impacting all equipment for communication, control and computer applications, since the increased signal-processing speed will basically influence how systems could and should be designed.

At the outset, it is recognized that the broad technology base needed to support this project is pushing the current frontier. It is also clear that progress must be achieved from the creativity of many contributors who are single-minded in their convictions, but broad-minded enough to want their convictions challenged and their conclusions altered or confirmed. Indeed, the project is designed accordingly. The organization and method of operation are both part of the experiment.

We must work with outside organizations; if we attempt to do everything ourselves, it will cost us at least three times more. Besides, we need ideas from people working in several different organizations.

The other benefit for the corporation for initiating and staging this program is to have a resident group of well-connected experts who serve as the company's own think tank. The benefits for all participants are their involvement, mutual interaction, and, above all, another significant perspective of their own roles.

Dr. Omni then proceeded rapidly through a list of enabling technologies and gave a sample list of individual projects from basic research through to speculative new projects involving new concepts. He demonstrated how these were time-sequenced and mutually interactive.

"Please note this particular example of the interplay between longer-term and nearer-term applications. In the optoelectronics technology project, two specific areas will have immediate near-term impact. One is on the modelling and simulation of optoelectronics devices. This highlights similar issues in current silicon VLSI circuits. The importance of recognizing the more basic limitations can be used to identify and classify the relative values of certain current activities in VLSI. This is very helpful since effectiveness of VLSI research is important when a large amount of funding is devoted to this task. The other is on improving the fabrication technology based on MOCVD. The longer-term investigation is on improving this technique which is already currently being used in our production facility."

The CEO commended Dr. Omni for the excellent presentation and left him with one action item. "Please submit your new R&D plan to me in two weeks for my formal approval, after settling the remaining issues with the other department directors."

This imaginary scene at Everything Inc., together with the Xany story, illustrates the roles of R&D and of production in high-technology related businesses. In a large organization, an internal team, knowledgeable about the business of the company and the relevant technology, is needed to enable business decisions to be made without exposing the company to undue technology-related risks. In Xany, a specialized company, its technology and its business are intimately related. In both cases the requirement is for an intelligent database which exists and is being paid for. Everything Inc. invests in the R&D team while Xany's management has made investments in themselves. Xany's operation could take place at a large corporation. Dr. Xan would be a speculative product manager. The apparent difference is created by the illusion that Dr. Xan has no R&D cost. However, in the large company at the product-planning stage, the situation is identical. If Dr. Xan's previous research cost is totally factored into the cost of the project, then Everything Inc. will be in a non-competitive situation. However, the value of Dr. Xan's previous research experience should presumably benefit other projects. The attributable cost should be relatively minor.

We can readily see how research and development are vital in many types of business. Moreover, production should be singled out for careful examination. Technology impacts greatly on the way research, development and production should be conducted. They play primary roles in determining the competitiveness of a product or service in the marketplace and, therefore, its success or failure. Even the accounting procedures used in deriving and distributing R&D costs can have serious consequences on the profitability of a given product or service.

Chapter 9

Technology Transfer

A panel discussion on technology transfer is about to begin at a conference. On the stage sitting behind their individual microphones are eight panelists. At one table are representatives of transferrers and at another, those of transferees: the givers and the recipients. To provide a balanced and all-embracing coverage of the topic from every aspect, a technologist, a businessman, a politician, and an economist have been invited to talk for each side. The usual mixed audience fills the hall.

The Chairman of the session calls the meeting to order and announces the format of the discussion. It is to be a seven-minute prepared statement from each of the panelists. The audience is requested to raise questions and issues after listening to all the presentations.

Before calling on the first speaker, the Chairman, a distinguished journalist, begins with a preamble.

"Ladies and Gentlemen, and Members of the panel, I was asked by the Conference Program Chairman to organize this panel discussion in order to bring out the key features that could influence the success or failure of any form of technology transfer taking place in this world. He also reminded me that the discussion should be steered towards identifying the new difficulties faced by all of us who are engaged in this field. One such difficulty is the rapid development of an over-abundance of sophisticated and interdependent technologies. It turned out to be a fun task. I have enjoyed every minute of working with these eight panelists over the last several months. I am sure you'll be stimulated by their presentations and you will be eager to add your contributions to this fascinating and complex subject. Let me call upon Dr. Knowall to kick off with his presentation. Dr. Knowall is a renowned technologist, trained as an electronics engineer, and he has a wide range of scientific and technological achievements. He has been involved in several cases of technology transfers and has recently been asssigned to chair a Presidential Committee on Technology Transfer Policy. Ladies and Gentlemen, Dr. Knowall."

Dr. Knowall is a thoughtful man, true to his professional training as an engineer. He is pragmatic, and yet precise. He seldom minces his words. He rises, walks to center stage where the overhead projector is, switches the machine on, and puts the first viewgraph up. It reads in bold letters, "TECHNOLOGY TRANSFER," but across these words is a red line indicating that the title has been canceled. He begins.

"Mr. Chairman, Ladies and Gentlemen, permit me to dive immediately into this serious discussion. Technoloogy transfer is a misnomer. That is why I put a thin red line through my first viewgraph. The word, transfer, implies a simple act of passing something from one party to another. In the case of making technology work for a specific task, it involves many factors. It is not a single act of transfer. It always involves preparation, infrastructure building, learning, and adaptation."

As he speaks, he slips his second viewgraph into position. It is a bar chart with the words "preparation, infrastructure building, etc." as a list, with a bar of a certain length marked with a time scale following each of the words. It shows that preparation starts first. The other activities begin at different times and for various time spans. He continues.

"Even the word, technology, is not really appropriate. It is too generic and can give people the idea that the transfer process applies universally to any technology. I prefer to use a long specific description for each technology-transfer endeavor. This point will be made clearer in my talk. I did not cross off the name 'Technology Transfer' in a bold red line because any generic name has problems. I merely like to alert you to the lack of precision of this title. It is a convenient shorthand description of a collection of complex processes.

"The time scale on my second viewgraph for each of the activity areas is different for a specific task, while the work involved is also varied. Preparation could involve simply a policy decision of buying a laser cloth-cutting machine for a garment factory. It could mean a full-scale study of the farming industry of a country to assess how and what biotechnology-based horticulture technology could be imported and adapted to local use. My list of activities can and must be particularized for a given technology-transfer task.

"Even though I am extremely conscious of the broad implications of a technology-transfer process in areas other than the pure technology aspects, I shall confine my discussion to the science and technology portion. Summarized in matrix forms, the next two viewgraphs show the classification of the technology-transfer processes. The first shows that from concept through design to product, the steps embrace theory, research, development and engineering. Across any of the squares, a technology-transfer process is needed. Each can be quantified in terms of cost and duration. A qualitative description may help to define the degree of interaction required between the transferrers and transferees. The second shows that, as technology-transfer tasks move from turn-key through adaptation, to design and innovation, complete infrastructures of training are needed to educate personnel to undertake production, development, research and education. This viewgraph is to be interpreted thus: for a turn-key job, only training of production operators are needed, while for achieving innovation associated with a technology, educators, researchers, development and production engineers must be available. In other words, technology transfer involves the build-up of a training system for knowledge and skill transfer.

"Having defined the basis of technology transfer, I am now ready to outline for you my view of the challenges we face in current technology-transfer processes. In our state of technological abundance, products invariably utilize a host of different technologies and product cycles are short. In any single case, we are dealing with multiple technology transfers and requiring an assortment of infrastructures. Take the case of a turn-key transfer of an automatic multipurpose drilling machine for a company making printed circuit boards. As soon as this machine is in place and running, the plant supervisor finds that he needs a much more knowledgeable operator who is not afraid of learning to read and interpret system manuals, so that the machine can be used efficiently. He should worry about the maintenance support given by the supplier, since any downtime of this machine can disrupt his production schedule very significantly. The drill bits are much more expensive and cannot be sharpened on his usual grinding wheels. Even the lubricant for this machine is different from that used on his other machines. Job scheduling must be rescheduled to fit around this new acquisition. His life is suddenly and rudely altered.

"For a design-oriented case such as the Application Specific Integrated Circuit (ASIC), in the semi-conductor technology area, the overall process of transfer is very complex. Even for the technology alone, the trained manpower needed in the infrastructure is formidable. This field is moving at a rapid pace. For every technological improvement in semi-conductor technology, the changes to the ASIC design procedure could be very extensive, and new technology transfer is required. The major implication in such a case of technology transfer is its never-ending nature once the process is started; otherwise, the initial investment of money and effort is soon wasted as obsolescence sets in.

"As a technologist working on the side of the transferrer, I'd like to conclude by stating my incentives for being willing to do technology export. My final viewgraph lists the major reasons. In the age of interdependence, strategic links must be formed to share the huge cost involved. There are so many facets in the technology puzzle that have to be in place. Strategic linkages are the piecing together of the expertise to form a whole. In such an alliance, everyone is a winner. In the age of abundance, new technology cannot easily be developed in a back room and then sprung on the market when it is completed. There are real dangers of its being insufficiently different from and less attractive than other solutions that surely are emerging in the meantime. By exporting the ideas at an early stage, one is, as it were, creating one's own bandwagon by encouraging people to strategically align with oneself.

"I am also willing to negotiate transfers of well-established technologies, especially those that could be adapted to take advantage of the environment existing in the transferee's base. The sweetener that I can offer is my solid experience base. The advantages for me could be from many directions. I may like to move on to another technology and be ready to cover my new investment with the capital realized by the transfer. I may be looking for means to reduce operating costs by moving the major cost component of that technology to an area where that component cost is lower. I may simply be running a technology-transfer business. For whatever the reason, the process of transfer must be carried out with meticulous attention to all details. From the technology angle, the easiest mistake might be one of not knowing all the technological support assumed to be available at the recipients' home ground. Thank you for your attention."

The Chairman duly thanks Dr. Knowall for not exceeding his allotted time and proceeds to call on Mr. Buck, a prosperous businessman and the CEO of a broker firm in technology transfer. He informs the audience that Mr. Buck is a Harvard MBA graduate and has a scientific background. Mr. Buck is well known as the globe-trotting deal maker. Many developing nations regard him as almost a savior.

Mr. Buck shows a sequence of slides of chemical plants in Calcutta, high-yield rice farms in India, a radio assembly plant in Mozambique, interspersed with beautiful scenic slides of exotic places around the world. It is like taking a whirlwind trip around the tourist world. He starts his narrative without visual aids.

"Ladies and Gentlemen, technology transfer is rewarding. It is like the gentle rain from heaven above. It is twice blessed. It blesses both the transferrer and the transferee. What the slides showed were pictorial examples from the past. The industrial age touched the lives of people around the world rather like a tidal wave. It started in Europe and spread out to the nether parts of the world. It was like the handing down of old clothes from the firstborn to his younger siblings until there was little left for handing down. When the post-industrial age came to the developed nations, many others were still only beginning the industrial age. Socio-political events, however, marched faster than the natural tide of the industrial revolution. As a result, the developing nations sought to accelerate their progress through technology transfers. A turn-key operation enables a country without a plastic industry to import a complete chemical plant to make, say, polyvinyl chloride (PVC). All of a sudden, this country could make many plastic parts for utensils, electrical wire, etc. This developing nation is attempting to leapfrog the technological barrier. I am like Cupid making sure that the right knots are tied. I go around the world to seek the lonely hearts, understand their hidden wishes, and then fire the right arrows. There are still a lot of seekers and givers around, but I have recently discovered my second pair of wings. Technology transfer is now important among corporate giants. Strategic alliances, as Dr. Knowall mentioned earlier, are now necessary for competitive reasons. The cost of technology development is so huge that no one is big enough to afford making the investment. This situation is made worse by the archaic antitrust laws, especially in the U.S.A. I guess that technology-transfer specialists will be created internally within corporations to look after the various transfer processes from concept to products.

"Let me expand on the theme of strategic alliances. This is a different game from matching two parties for a straightforward turn-key technology-transfer job. There, the transferrer is supposed to have all the knowledge, experience and know-how of the technology he is offering for transfer. The recipient expects to be in business as soon as the transfer process is completed. Here, in forming strategic alliances, both parties recognize the importance of pooling certain technology resources in order to cover the vast technological areas from which some or all of their products derive their competitive advantages.

"This type of transaction is full of conflicts. The companies traditionally guard their technology bases jealously. Even when it becomes obvious that the R&D investments required for sustaining the competitiveness of a product line are too large to be justifiable on a ROI basis, companies are still reluctant to share what they regard as their proprietary and critical technologies. For example, a semiconductor company pours money into developing a fabrication process for microprocessors based on one technical approach. Its confidence may be poorly placed. The progress of technology in this area is along a broad front. One of these companies could be the outright winner in two to three years and may hold that position for a few years. Under this scenario, a flexible approach, even if it feels like selling one's soul by making an alliance and hedging the bet, makes a lot of sense.

"My job is to look for areas of technology that are developing rapidly, and that are keys to many industrial and business developments. Again, as matchmaker, I coax reluctant parties to get to know each other. In this age of sex equality, there is no need to distinguish who is the bride or who is the groom. All I should provide are the rudimentary attractions of all pertinent details why a consummation could result in bonnie offsprings. The most frequently used technique is the carrot-and-stick trick. For fast-moving and broad-based technologies, the missed opportunities can be both the carrot and the stick. For complementary technologies, the attraction is for broadening the technology base. For complementary application ranges of a single technology, the stick is the threat of intrusion by one's complementary business colleagues. A good example here is the acquisition of telecommunication companies by computer companies and *vice versa*. These two industries are, as yet, not making strategic alliances even if they should. They are determined to remain single.

"Technology transfer for strategic alliances must be organized with a continuing timetable. The technologies involved are not in a matured state. There is an expectation that continuous progress will be made over a significant period of time. Shared rights for intellectual properties generated through this joint effort must be clearly defined. Effective exchange of information on a continuing basis and at many different working levels must be agreed upon and organized accordingly. The freer an approach, the more recognition for the need of both complementary and overlapping tasks, the simpler it would be for an easier and fruitful relationship. The level of competence of the parties concerned must be reasonably on par with each other. Management of professional jealousy is imperative.

"My past experiences can be summed up in a sentence. I make technology work for us. From this angle, there is another component of my technology-transfer business. I believe that I can transfer to a business environment, and lead, a team responsible for the development of a promising technology. I can be the venture capitalist to fund this team with the necessary capital and management guidance. When technologies are as interrelated and as abundant as those which exist today, I am the marriage broker who can be the venture capitalist, the consultant, the planner, and the logistics expert to generate happy and prosperous new hybrid families. I believe that my service is indispensable in the technology-transfer role. Thank you for lending me your ears."

The audience applaud in appreciation. The Chairman politely bows. He announces,

"The next speaker needs no introduction. He is none other than our Minister of Trade and Industries. Mr. Smart has agreed to come to our conference in spite of his busy schedule and to talk as an individual and not as a government spokesman. When there has been so much talk about restrictive practices in trade and export control, I appreciate his offer of not speaking in his official capacity. Mr. Smart graduated as a Public Administration major. His career spanned both the private and public sectors. He is responsible for the recent narrowing of our trade gap. Ladies and Gentlemen, Mr. Alexander Smart."

"Good morning, Mr. Chairman. With your permission, I will first show a short film of three minutes. I am particularly struck by the work of this global thinker who has brilliantly put his thoughts into the form of a movie. The title is 'The Hand That Feeds'."

The light in the hall darkens. The screen flickers into life. A blinding flash as a nuclear device detonates and the awesome barrel-like drum of deadly smoke rises from the epicenter. The next scene is equally powerful. A giant rocket with the space shuttle attached to it rises majestically from the launch pad at Cape Canaveral. The accompanying music lifts the spirit of the audience to a great height. Abruptly, the sound of a low howling wind cuts across the hall. On the screen are starving refugees in a desert setting. Bones protruding, half-clothed men, women and children are sitting idly around. Alternately, the scene switches from this land of desolation to the mighty Aswan Dam. The camera selectively shows dying babies in the arms of withered mothers and the tranquil and rich upper reaches of the Nile, the power of huge water turbines for electricity generation at the Dam and then again the desert. Soon the scene changes to bustling Tokyo and the inside of a spick-and-span robot-controlled assembly line of a typical Japanese factory, neat, clinical and efficient. In contrast, the next scene is that of a sweat shop with perspiring laborers in a cotton mill somewhere. The film ends with a pictorial essay of a day in the life of an ordinary family of four, portraying work, study and leisure. The only spoken words come at the very end in the form of a rhetorical question: Is technology the hand that feeds?

As the audience tries to make themselves present in mind and spirit, Mr. Smart steps onto the rostrum and addresses the audience,

"Ladies and Gentlemen, is technology the hand that feeds? What I like about this film is the richness of the messages it delivers to each of us individually. To me, it certainly says that technology is almighty but that it must be used carefully for the benefit of our society. Mishandling or a lack of understanding of the consequences of technology and its usage can be disastrous.

"The Aswan Dam was an epoch-making project of Egypt. Egypt, after an illustrious early civilization, was languishing. Progress around the world bypassed her. After World War II, Egypt was led by strong leaders who wished to reconstruct the country with vigor. The Aswan project was born in the belief that, with plenty of low-cost electrical power, much expansion of productive efforts could be sustained. Hydroelectric power was a mature technology and so was dam building. Politically, it was a convenient and popular move. No one, however, was aware of the ecological effects the Dam would cause. During the long years of building the Dam, Egypt was in debt. The relocation of many villages along the banks of the Nile caused social problems. An international effort was mounted to move one of the most important ancient monuments to prevent it from being submerged to oblivion. The construction was hindered by internal strife. When finally the Dam was completed, the benefit it brought was found to be less significant than originally expected. It turns out that the ecological consequences are severe. The large expanse of water upstream altered the weather pattern over the entire reaches of the Nile River, a river that had sustained life in Egypt for thousands of years. There is now a threat of the Sahara Desert expanding to engulf millions of acres of rich arable land. Even the lives of the birds and insects are forever disturbed. Gone are the marshlands and the flood plains that sustained the myriad of life forms. Vanished are the habitats for the birds and the wild animals. The Aswan Dam is a technology transfer that has long lasting complications.

"On a national basis, technology transfer can help in the ways already mentioned by the two speakers before me. A developing nation can catch up faster while a developed nation can benefit from an expanded market, not only through unloading mature technology, but also through the increased buying power of the developing countries as their economies grow more robust. On a global basis, it is like a mutual help arrangement. The problems are difficult to foresee. Over-zealousness should be avoided. We must try very hard to avoid examples such as the Aswan Dam.

"Technologies are now very powerful. International control of certain technologies are necessary in order to preserve the balance of power. A group of insurgents can hold the world to ransom with chemical or biological weapons, or a nuclear bomb or two. Yet for promoting trade and industries, technology exchanges and transfers must be encouraged. I strongly believe that the only way to solve these implicit problems is through education and through mutual assistance. The global village is too small now to tolerate large discrepancies in life even if the living standards need not be uniformly high. The mutual help through technology transfer must be fostered and accelerated. We must aim to raise the productivity per capita on a global scale. In fact, that is the message as I read it from the film we have just seen. Thank you."

The audience is moved considerably by the arguments presented by the Minister of Trade and Industries. Mr. Smart has alerted many of the listeners to the way in which politics invariably creeps into the picture of what otherwise is a mere technology problem. The Chairman says nothing for about twenty seconds in order that the pregnant silence may sink in. He announces at last that the final speaker speaking on behalf of the transferrers is Professor Figures, a Professor of Economics at the local university. Professor Christopher Figures pioneered a theory of the Gain Mechanism in Technology Transfer.

The gain is directly attributable to the additional productive work any technology-transfer process involves.

"Mr. Chairman, Ladies and Gentlemen, I shall concentrate today on the economic value attributable to any technology transfer. I shall not be speaking on the Gain Mechanism except in passing. My talk is based in part on an extensive article written by J.L. Enos, published in the *Asian-Pacific Economic Literature*, March 1989, entitled, 'Transfer of Technology.'

"Any technology has intrinsic values. From conception to a matured state much work has been added to the basic idea. This can be considered as an accumulated cost. During this period the technology is employed to reduce the cost of products or to increase the added value of products. The total differential costs can be subtracted from the accumulated cost to generate the current value of this technology from the transferrer's viewpoint. He can set a selling price by adding his due profit, and hope that someone will want to be the recipient of this technology through a transfer process. In most practical cases both the intrinsic value and the differential costs are incurred by a succession of not necessarily related people or enterprises. As a result, this method of cost estimation is only of theoretical interest.

"The transaction price is based (1) on a perceived value of the importance of a technology to the recipient and, hence, how much the recipient is willing to pay, and (2) on the compensation the transferrer feels appropriate for giving away the hard-gained experience and know-how. They may bear little resemblance to the actual costs involved. The whole transaction is based on the projected benefits and greed. No one ever appears to be totally satisfied with the technology-transfer process. Eternal arguments are common, especially over the price paid.

"To understand the difficulty of evaluating technology transfer in economic terms, it is necessary to look at the data from the historical viewpoints of past cases. These are comparatively simple ones. Even then they involve: direct foreiggn investment, jooint ventures, non-equity investment, licensing, franchising, technical consultancy, capital goods purchase, etc. The technologies range from innovation, to rapidly improving, to slowly improving, to matured. These two lists can be used as the labeling parameters along the x-y axes of a graph respectively. Actual cases can be inserted at the intersections of the most appropriate pairs of parameters to show whatever associations might be significant. In fact, cases are dotted rather widely over the entire graph paper, indicating the wide range of different driving forces for these technology-transfer cases.

"In the technology intensive societies, technology transfers are taking place for many more elusive reasons and for an increasing number of technologies at different stages of development. The only thing an economist can say about the subject is, quoting Enos, 'The nature of technology transfer established itself quickly. It has a natural coherence and is an important issue.' Studies have shown that no significant conclusions can be drawn until some measurement of success can be formulated. Even then, development economists would argue that interrelationships exist between the application of scarce technical and management resources and the narrowing of economic activities. Thus, the apparent successes could mask failures in missed opportunities.

"One measurement is the total factor productivity growth (TFPG). It is the fraction of a nation's or company's growth that is not at-tributable to increases in the quantities of inputs, such as labor and capital. This measures indirectly the effect of the technology transfer. It is probably the best we can do. Other measures are even more indirect and rely on rather soft assumptions. The conclusion Enos drew is stated as follows: 'Presumably there are some general prin-ciples, valid across countries, technologies and time. If there are such principles, they have escaped our discovery until now.' It is an un-answered challenge.

"My Gain Mechanism Theory is a step-by-step approach to com-pute the gain in economic terms at every stage of a technology-transfer process. For each stage an economic agent or agents can be identified along with the mechanism or mechanisms involved in the process. In this manner a deeper understanding can be derived for any specific case. This technique can be applied to all types of transfer cases and to an arbitrary degree of refinement. The transfer of a conceptual idea into a research project can be equated to a cost or negative gain, while the transfer of a research project into an externally funded development project can be equated to an income or gain. The economic agent involved in both of these stages of transfer is simply the loaded cost of the people engaged in these processes. For a complex case of technology transfer, such as from a matured technology to an operating manufacturing plant, this can be dealt with simply as an investment analysis or it can be analyzed to different levels of detail through constructing a relational network or tree. Variability becomes large and the analysis is more subjective and is reduced to an art rather than a science. I am afraid that the Gain Mechanism Theory might just be a useful tool rather than the solution.

"There is a joke about us, the economists. We always have answers to problems, but the answers may not provide the solution to the problems. Thank you for listening to my answers."

After listening to three talks, the audience is already flaking out a bit. This heavy dosage of economic mumbo jumbo in the fourth talk is sufficient to send some of them to soothing slumberland. The Chairman stays alert. He cannot be otherwise. He promptly thanks the Professor and declares a short break in preparation for a change of direction in the discussion. After a coffee break of fifteen minutes, he announces the next speaker. Dr. Charma is an old-timer in the technology transfer. He works for the Chamber of Commerce and has already accumulated thirty years of service.

He has seen India's technology base grow from a little above zero to one that is almost self-sufficient. Most of this growth has been linked to technology-transfer efforts.

"Mr. Chairman, my Ladies and Gentlemen. This conference reminds me of being at a debating event. Yet we are not really taking opposite views; only views from different angles. I am going to trace through various stages of technology transfers with a number of key examples. Let us go right back in history to the days before I was born; to the days when India was under British rule. Railway systems were built with local labor under the supervision of British engineers and foremen. The steel railway tracks came from England and so did the locomotives and carriages. The only technology transfers that occurred were the instructions received by the laborers on how to sweat and toil over preparing the ground and laying the tracks. It was really an investment exercise by a colonial power. Yet, the railway systems contributed towards the opening up of India.

"By the time India became an independent nation, a fabric of basic industries was left behind by Britain. India, having received little guidance and having not been educated to a level of competency necessary to independently operate and maintain these industries, quickly encountered difficulties in keeping everything going. Ignorance and pride made the situation worse. The joy of independence soon changed to despair. The legacy of transplanted industries was not exactly helpful. It was to take many years for India to rebuild from scratch, a step at a time, towards a truly independent nation. During this process meaningful technology transfers were used as one of the means to bridge the technology gap.

"I was entering university at the time of independence. My youthful enthusiasm was fired by the exhilarating new nationhood. I went to the classes with a great deal of expectation and loved the esoteric stuff that the professors delivered to the wide-eyed youths. 'You will know more than your counterparts in England when you finish my course. I am bringing the most up-to-date and complete knowledge for you,' proudly proclaimed the Oxbridge-trained Indian dons. To be fair, they were great teachers and very learned. I was one of the top students and I received a free trip for industrial training in England as my graduation prize. It was at the factory that I was humbled. I suddenly realized that the bookwork, so neat and logical that I could reproduce it with ease, was not sufficient for me even to start a real life design. I did not know that there was a real world out there. A technician, whom I initially thought was a bit of dirt, turned out to be my savior. He was my guru. He taught me that learning from life is every bit as important as from books. He gave me the insight that a range of different skills and knowledge were needed to carry out a task. He gave me the insight that successful technology transfer involved having on tap a whole host of related skills and knowledge. In other words, a complete infrastructure of relevant resources must be present.

"Before a successful textile yarn factory can be established by the importation of a number of spinning machines, it is important to understand how the machines operate and how they are maintained. The supply and the quality of raw materials must match the quantity and type of thread that the machines can produce. What must be done if the thread breaks? What lubrication oil must be purchased for keeping the machine working, etc.

"Over the years, I learned to ask for many things whenever a technology transfer is contemplated. These things all could be discovered by asking the question, 'Do we have the needed infrastructure?' To get the answers, we test the availability of everything we can conceive of that may be required. We then ask the transferrer to tell us where he gets all the supplies that are needed to run the equipment. This can be very revealing and serves as a check against our own estimations. For complex technology transfer tasks, the level of understanding of both the transferrer and the transferee is at a higher plane. The validation that all necessary infrastructures are present can be performed more knowingly. Meticulous care is still highly recommended. This process must be understood thoroughly, not only because the success of the transfer process is at stake, but also because the price tag for this technology could be right for one customer but very wrong for another. Caveat emptor applies here with a vengeance and it is not because the seller is cheating.

"To improve rice yield, technology transfer from the International Rice Research Institute (IRRI) to India proved to be more difficult than it first appeared. IRRI found that the lack of a bureaucratic support system and the presence of determined policy-makers were the principal causes for not attaining a high level of success. We in India were not as convinced, but decided to strengthen our support system anyway.

"Technology transfer in matured technologies such as steel making, cement and textile machinery brought a great deal of benefit to India. I attribute this to be related to the state of development of India. We had all the necessary infrastructure in place to deal with these technology transfers in each of these cases. Now we are considering the transfer of fiber optics technology and the semiconductor silicon IC technology—specifically, optical fiber waveguide fabrication and ASIC technology. We need optical fibers for building a new communication network to criss-cross the entire subcontinent. With millions of kilometers of fiber needed, local manufacturing appears to be essential. The preliminary findings are not too encouraging: we have no infrastructure to support fiber fabrication that gives sufficient value addition. We have to import almost all the raw materials. The energy cost is high. We lack precision rotational machines. We have no local suppliers of sophisticated dimension measurement equipment makers. As we are unlikely to manufacture such equipment, we may decide to import the fiber waveguides and to assemble them into suitable cable structures. Here we already have a cable-making capability for electrical cables. The manufacturing procedures are similar. We are now looking into the critical differences and trying to quantify whether the completed and tested products can compete with imported products. Even if this should be a negative profit-generating decision, the saving of the telecommmunication cable industry from destruction could be a deciding factor.

"Everyone has considered at one time or another the development of an IC technology base. IC's are the integral part of any electronic equipment. It is predicted that without a source of IC supply no one can be in the electronics equipment business. It has also been shown that the total investment needed to establish the complete infrastructure to support a semi-conductor IC industry is in the order of billions of dollars. In addition the continued injection of new investment to keep pace with the progress of this technology is in the order of 8% of the turnover. Even the giants of this industry are making strategic alliances in order to stay competitive without over-investment in R&D. We are wise to these facts and we are consider-ing only the ASIC of silicon bipolar technology. We argue that tailored circuits are always needed since variety is the spice of life. We also contend that signal processing will be at very high speeds. For achieving circuits with equal high-speed performance, we have to decide whether the simpler MOS technology with more difficult lithographic technology should be chosen over the more complex bipolar technology with a less-exacting lithographic requirement.

"I am sure you can see that for a technology transferee, the considerations are numerous. As far as we are concerned the transfer-rer is sitting pretty there. They just have to name their price. On the other hand, I can sense that the situation is more complex, especially when the transferrer is looking for partners in order to lengthen the life of a fast obsolescing technology. This situation is likely to worsen as technology sophistication becomes even more pronounced. The network of interrelated support infrastructures will snare everyone.

"'It was the best of times, it was the worst of times, it was the age of wisdom, it was epoch of incredulity.' These words of Charles Dickens apply well to the situation of technology and its transferen-ces. It is also a clear revelation that abundance of choice is a double-edged sword. I hope that you have enjoyed listening as much as I have enjoyed giving this talk. Thank you."

"This guy is interesting. At the beginning I thought he must really be living in the last century. He is remarkably up-to-date," one mem-ber of the audience realizes.

The Chairman, in his usual way, thanks the speaker and proceeds to introduced the next businessman from Singapore. He has a joint venture company making a cosmetic product. Amongst his products is a wrinkle-removing facial cream that is based on the use of a skin-absorbing variety of B-12 vitamin, and a magic hair restorer that works on the principle that hair follicles will grow when the nutrient supply is exactly right. He has worked for a multinational cosmetic company and has good contacts with some of the best biotechnologists in the world. He is also well connected with the Pacific Rim investment community.

"The Chairman asked me to share with you my experience of technology transfer. I thought he was kidding. I replied that I might be into technology, but I am only a businessman trying to put together a winning package. He said that he might be confusing me by using the term technology transfer inappropriately. He said that it would be fine if I talked about how I put together my newest joint venture company in cosmetic products. He assured me that it would be an excellent example of validating success in what he termed technology transfer. After listening to the previous speakers, I am now persuaded that I can call my effort a case of technology transfer.

"Two years ago I was talking to a physiologist friend of mine. He told me that Vitamin B-12 deficiency causes skin to lose elasticity. He was searching for a method to measure skin elasticity so that he could detect B-12 vitamin deficiency. On that day he was very excited because an electronic engineer colleague at his university came up with an ingenious solution. As it turned out, I was exploring at that time the possibility of establishing a subsidiary company in Asia for a multinational cosmetic company. The question flashed through my mind that if a facial cream has B-12 in it, would the skin absorb B-12 and increase elasticity immediately? If this were possible, would wrinkles just disappear?

"I realized then that I was on to something significant. I changed my task of setting up a subsidiary company to one of forming a joint venture company involving the use of the know-how of the parent company for making the base part of the product and then adding value to it through innovation. In this case the innovation required some R&D investment. Now I really have the best of both worlds. Standard products and assured markets from the parent company serve as the bread-and-butter lines, while the innovative new products add strength and continuity to our product lines. In addition, I am in a position to take a better equity position in the company.

"The search for a skin-absorbed B-12 vitamin material turned out to be rather tricky. Luckily, through my contacts in the budding biotechnology world, I was able to persuade a brilliant entrepreneurial scientist to do the necessary preparatory investigations. He was able to provide sufficient evidence for me to convince my multinational partner to accept the joint venture proposal. Singapore was ideal for siting this new company. The Government of Singapore offers the right incentives for such a high-technology venture. The existence of the Molecular Biotechnology Centre (MBC), a multi-million-dollar research entity at the University of Singapore is another key factor that swayed our decision in Singapore's favor. After a year's work, carried out by investigators at the MBC under our sponsorship, they have succeeded in transforming the known candidate materials of B-12 to one that is soluble in the fatty acid base of the cosmetic cream and which at the same time remains actively interacting with the outer skin cells, resulting in the efficient absorption of B-12 through the dermal cells of the skin. I regard this as a lucky break, but really it is a case of advanced technology transfer plus some original work. It is a thoroughly modern technology advancement.

"The hair lotion with a formula to encourage regrowth of dormant hair follicles is strictly a developmental task. We purchased the right to use the research result and proceeded to scale it up for production. Admittedly, we are still short of field results to validate the claims. We feel that a lotion which is intrinsically kind to the hair may have a chance of increasing hair growth and it should appeal to many balding men. We have decided to be strictly honest in our claims. We are selling it as a hair tonic that bastes hair in the pristine environment generated naturally by the body to protect the growth of hair. This man-made lotion supplements that produced naturally and thereby offers improved protection against the harsh environment to which we are exposed. In the process the follicles are more likely to succeed in developing healthy hairs. We are organizing controlled groups of users who will be given the opportunity to buy the lotions at a substantial discount. They are encouraged to provide their comments to us, particularly if a thickening growth of hair is observed. We are doing further refinement work on the composition of the lotion. We are trying to establish whether there are differences in the composition of the natural oils belonging to people with little tendency to lose hair prematurely and of those that do have thinning thatches. I suppose this is the sort of technology transfer that occurs often in a company with its own research laboratory and development area.

"In Singapore many companies are subsidiaries of major national and transnational corporations. Singapore has educated its manpower appropriately to serve the needs of every level of operations and has set up various financial, communication, transport, technical and research support structures in anticipation of the need of certain targeted high-value-added manufacturing activities. We found it attractive enough to locate ourselves there. This joint venture company comes with standard cosmetics production facilities and innovative results as a result of research that has been started elsewhere. Singapore derives employment benefits, income from the services provided and a gradual strengthening of its own technology base. Already more local brand-name products are appearing. It is an example of using technology transfer indirectly for the upgrading of a national economy.

"Is this a form of strategic alliance? I believe it is one of the successful forms in which unequal partners both derive benefits. Both operate with a great deal of autonomy, but their joint effort is dovetailed. It is a remarkable win-win situation. I'd like to conclude by wishing all of you happy hunting for strategic alliances."

The next speaker is a tall, distinguished-looking politician. In his flowing national costume, he commands presence. A princely figure moves to the center stage.

"Mr. Chairman, it is a great privilege for me to be here among many distinguished experts. Ladies and gentlemen of the audience, I am a career diplomat and I speak today as a representative of a group of less-developed nations. With due respect to my fellow speakers, I am obliged to speak plainly about facts. What I see in technology transfers are unfair trading practices, exploitations, extortions and, at best, misplaced charities. Forgive me for being blunt, but let us look at the facts.

"During the dark days of slavery, the African continent was raided by unscrupulous slave traders. A huge number of able-bodied people were herded to various places around the world and put to work on the farms and plantations. Can you hear the sad songs of despair sung with such nobility and dignity? 'Ol' Man River he keeps on rolling along. I'm coming, I'm coming, for my head is bending low. I hear those gentle voices calling, Old Black Joe.' We can ask questions such as: Have they not been transported to a land of freedom? Is it an unalienable right for all men to have liberty and the pursuit of happiness? Are all men created equal? It took a bloody civil war and many years of struggle for civil rights before the Blacks in America secured equal legal status in U.S.A.

"The majestic landscape of the imposing Kilimanjaro and the mighty Victoria Falls are on the northern edges of the lush and fertile land now known as South Africa. Britain and the Dutch colonized it and fought over it. The Afrikaans, Dutch descendants, claimed their sovereign rights over it. They transplanted European technology and ruled with an iron fist. To ensure their supremacy they introduced the policy known as Apartheid, separation of development. Apartheid was touted as the most humane way of acknowledging the rights of the natives. Since the natives were said to be at a different stage of development and were less civilized, they must be trained step by step in their own course of development. This sounded rational enough except for the fact that the natives were not given the already claimed fertile lands. They were given only rudimentary education. They were a disadvantaged class.

"In the jungles of the Amazon, huge bull-dozers are busily

working even today clearing the rain forests. The imported technology is effectively creating wealth for a few. Even with the warning of the concerned environment preservation experts that such large-scale deforestation is disturbing the balance of ecology in the Amazon region, and even with concerned citizens organizing ordered resistance, the destruction is continuing. The results could be the breaking of the food chain and a consequent disaster for the primitive tribes in that region. Indeed, the results threaten the CO_2 balance and could accelerate the worsening of the greenhouse effect and bring about a dooms-day scenario for the world.

"How many technology transfers to underdeveloped nations are taking place that are not motivated by profit-making motives of the transferrers rather than by the desire to help? Of course I do accept that a mutually profitable transaction is the best. In the circumstance, I am really calling for transferrers to understand their responsibilities. They should make clear to the transferee what the broad and specific implications are in the undertaking. It is important for the transferee to have no illusions or false hopes. It is also imperative that safety and pollution control rules be enforced even if human life may be valued differently. The Bhopal Disaster, of the accidental release of poisonous insecticide, could have been avoided. Sometimes it is the recipient of technology who turns a blind eye to dangers even when the dangers could lead to self-destruction. Personal ambitions particularly are prevalent in authoritarian governments.

"I understand the value of technology transfers. I like to encourage all underdeveloped nations to be on the alert for appropriate opportunities. I caution them to be careful and vigilant. It is a good idea to make one's low-cost labor available in the production process for the world and thereby to increase the productivity and the prosperity of the people. It is not a good idea if, in doing so, the future has been mortgaged and the shackle of permanent second class has been put in place. No one should expect others to be selfless, but no one can be helped unless one helps oneself.

"In my talk, I preached for fairness, not benevolence or charity. I am convinced that we have advanced sufficiently in civilization to prevent a reversion to the dog-eat-dog concepts of the early capitalist society. I wish you well in your endeavors."

The audience and the speakers are numb as if they are punch-drunk. This politician has increased the tension of the place several fold, and they all are hurt from the below-the-belt punches. Yet they sense the earnestness of this politician. They are incensed and vow to themselves to do their best lest they fall from grace. The Chairman regains his composure after the seventh speaker returns to his seat. The Chairman declares that the next speaker is to conclude the formal presentations by the panel members.

Professor Forecaster is another well-known economist. He is from the West Indies. His life-time study has been in the area of national economic development. The topic on which he is to speak is the importance of technology transfer to the recipient nations. He is to address the future rather than the past.

"Ladies and Gentlemen, let me start by letting into this discussion a big breath of fresh air. It is necessary to blow away the unpleasant scent that has permeated this room. Technology of the future will smell like roses. The varieties and names are countless, but they are all gorgeous and they all are intoxicating. They may have a myriad of thorns, but carefully handled, they will bring happiness and satisfaction for the grower and the recipient. The perfectly blossoming red rose buds are still the best expression of love any lady would treasure from the perfect gentleman.

"I see new technologies as inextricably intertwined with our lives as they are among themselves. Even in the West Indies where crystal-clear blue sea surrounds our idyllic islands and people just laze around on the soft, warm, invitingly white sand beach, we cannot do without our air-conditioned hotels with all the mod-cons. Guests would be insulted if the waiter produce a Singapore Sling made with our local rum. 'No coke' and 'no ice' will turn away almost all the American visitors. If our airports have no electronic landing systems, and if our airlines are without a computer booking system, we will miss much of the tourist trade. The consequence is a decrease in our GNP. The importation of the basic technology to enable the imported technological products to be maintained or serviced is essential. The situation is exponential. Its growth rate is proportional to its size. At the beginning, everything was hard to do. We were always short of this and that. All of a sudden, our horizon widened. We could do more ourselves and depend less on others.

"True, we are still a happy-go-lucky people. We grow our sugar cane, but we now have combined harvesters to help us. We still enjoy chewing the sugar cane and deftly trim and cut the long stalks with a curved knife. We still do a lot of wolf whistling when gorgeous ladies pass by in their latest swim suits. We still while away excitedly the four days of Test cricket at the grandstand, admiring the fine glance that sends the hard deep-red ball straight for four to the boundary, or a magnificent hook that the batter made to reach his first 'century,' or an impossible catch by the silly-mid-on to break a fine inning by a pair of cricketers.

"When we realized that the cost of importing compressed oxygen in bottle form to sell to scuba divers yields profits, we increased our effort to popularize this sport. It was a natural since we have clean sea water and colorful fishes. It soon dawned on us that we could make a lot more on each bottle sold if we have a liquid-oxygen storage tank or, even better, an oxygen-producing plant. Technology transfer is needed. Besides learning how to make oxygen on an industrial basis, we also discovered quality control. Our lackadaisical ways are definitely not acceptable when it comes to strict quality control. We quickly understand the dire consequences if a scuba diver suddenly runs out of oxygen due to an error in filling the oxygen bottle only half full. Worse still, if the bottle turns out to be filled with nitrogen. This can happen now in my country since we are making nitrogen as well as oxygen and are supplying our hospitals ourselves. We have progressed a long way through technology transfers in the industrial gas production area. In its wake we have assumed many new responsibilities. As I said, technology transfer is like a rose. If we handle it carefully, we can avoid being pricked and can enjoy the richness it brings.

"My economic theory of technology transfer in the future may be facetiously called 'Theory of the War of Roses.' It will last for a long time and it will have ups and downs. Emerging from it will be a winner, the one that can understand the nature of the economic problem at hand and the timely injection and careful handling of the processes of transfer.

"The theory is based on the premises that (1) an interwoven network of related infrastructure is needed to sustain a successful technology transfer, and (2) interdependence is ideal for accelerating the fulfillment of the mutual benefits. Hence, the theory states that technology transfer is an organic process essential for sustaining the future growth of the economy. Everyone must participate. It will be part and parcel of the free market-driven economy. Even though the less-developed nations regard technology transfers as a sort of lifeline for accelerating progress, the more advanced nations are well advised to participate in this process. The global village is reality.

"I come from a country with mixed cultures which almost drifted into existence. I often wonder about old countries with rich and enduring cultures that may not match the conditions imposed by the coming about of the global village. Take China, for instance. Her dynastic and authoritarian traditions have been partially responsible for the turmoil of the past eighty years, ever since the fall of the last Manchu Dynasty. Technology transfers with their increasing inter-dependence requirements may not be as fruitful as they could be. But life is an ongoing process and is never perfect. Only theoreticians dream about Utopia. Economists are contented when they can see a trend.

"Technology transfer, although narrower in scope and generally associated with applications, is synonymous with education. Its economic value cannot readily be separated out, though it is ap-parently obvious. It is a tool for improving productivity per capita.

Some organizations are more skilled in using it than others. Used incorrectly, it may even hinder the task at hand. In our age of rapid technological progress, the trend is to use this tool with increasing frequency and at all levels of our endeavors. Perhaps the way to express the economic value of technology transfer is to link it with the rate of growth of GNP. The measure of technology transfer could be pegged to the change in the Sales/RDE Expenditure ratio for manufacturing activities or in the Revenue/Capital Equipment Cost ratio for the service industry. This is a gross parameter with a slow response time. Over a period, the aggregate rise of this ratio is a good trend. It could be interpreted that technology transfers are producing positive effects in reducing the overall capital and labor cost.

"I do not think that I should be trying to develop an economic theory of technology transfer, *in situ*, at a conference. I would merely like to indicate the underlying thoughts on my approach to quantify a measure for the economic value of technology transfer. It is a great privilege to share my thoughts with you. Thank you."

Thus ends the formal presentations. It has taken just around an hour. What an hour it has been! The audience has been alternately electrified and calmed. All present are stimulated and during the talk had anxiously wanted to chip in, only to find that their unvoiced questions and opinions were addressed by one or other of the speakers. In the end they all feel more knowledgeable about the subject from the many different perspectives that the speakers have offered. When the Chairman announces that questions and contributions are welcome from the audience, there is no rush to the microphones placed for the convenience of the audience, one in each of the aisles between the blocks of seats.

"I am a supporter of the Green movement, and I'd like to applaud the speakers for putting the responsibilities of vigilance to environmental impacts and safety requirements fairly and squarely on those that are engaged in the business of technology transfer. In listening to the argument on technological interdependence and its implications for the global village, I am unclear as to where this will lead us. Are we being reduced to a homogeneous mass or, worse still, are we rapidly losing our freedom of choice?"

Dr. Forecaster indicates to the Chairman that he is prepared to respond.

"I cited China as an example to illustrate the difficulty she faces in adopting technology transfer in her environment. The catch 22 position is clear: if China goes alone, the wheels have all to be reinvented. This probably would mean a no-win situation for China to catch up with the rest of the world. If China participates in the technology-transfer process, then China must bridge the cultural gap of understanding the environment from whence the technology comes and make suitable accommodations to her own system to ensure the success of the transfer process. This could be interpreted as a watering down of an ideological position and hence unacceptable. From this angle, concept of the world village does lead to a discrimination against those systems that hinder progress. There is some loss of our freedom of choice."

Dr. Charma chips in: "No, no, we have no fear of becoming a homogeneous mass. On the contrary, we will have more choices than we ever wished in our age of abundance. Just to assure the questioner, let me tell you about the Theory of Chaos. This relatively new area of enquiry started when someone asked the following question. 'Can the small disturbance of air around a butterfly I see in my garden flapping its wings, result in the eventual formation of a hurricane that lashes the coast of Florida with winds up to 100 miles an hour?' It is now known that small changes can add up to unexpectedly large outcomes that trace many different paths along many different developmental routes. At the same time the detailed patterns often show regularities that exhibit similar appearances at any scale of enlargement. Thus, chaos is the result of systematic development in an environment with many independent small forces acting. When the number of variables are large, the paths of development are seemingly unpredictable. No matter how well we do our technology transfers, our environment, developed through history, will extract the benefit of these transferred technologies differently. My hunch says that if we take care of the more dominant aspects of a project, we will be well on the way to success. On the other hand, ideological inflexibility can easily become anathema to technology transfers, since science and technology require intellectual freedom to flourish."

A typical boffin type asks this question, "I am a researcher in science and I work at a university in a developed nation. As far as I can sense, no one cares about my work on an aspect of information theory. I have been searching for ways to classify the degrees of difficulties to break an encryptic message. I am excited about the mathematical relationships that can be used to express the order of complexity and I believe it to be a clue to understanding further the secret of better encryption. I have the feeling that even if I succeed, I'll be told by my engineering colleagues that whatever I propose may not be reducible to practice. 'Reduce to Practice' is a tiresome phrase. If my mathematics is elegant why worry about putting it to practice? I'd like to ask the panel whether any of the members worry about the interests of the individuals in the process of technology transfer."

Dr. Knowall beams at this opportunity to expound a bit about his pet topic: that the best result of a technology transfer is the passing on of the kernel of an idea or an essential fact. The next stage of development should be entrusted to those with the desire to utilize the idea or the fact. Of course the transfer can include the originator as part of the goodies delivered, particularly if he is not only an initiator but also has a bent for application.

"I am glad to hear your views on the beauty of scientific undertakings. I find, particularly in basic research laboratories, many people who share with you the view that you have just expressed. If it were the case, many ideas may be born to blush unseen in their full glory as they are not carefully nursed to maturity and expanded to the broadest generality. This type of work can only be undertaken by people with special talents like yourself. It is my contention that the most fruitful technology transfer involves a succession of talents at each stage of the transfer process. It is also my conviction that basic research becoming applied research is as much a technology transfer as a turn-key operation of transferring a piece of production equipment. Many a research laboratory for industry neglects the basic research aspect, since it makes no traceable impact on the bottom-line profit. I would advise CEOs to demand that at least 5% of basic research be conducted in-house. This would ensure that the coupling with the basic research community can be effectively maintained. After all, technology forecasting can be easier and the occasional realization of new business opportunities comes from new inventions."

Someone walks up to the microphone and announce herself as a company executive. She asks, "Is strategic alliance a myth? In view of the super-abundance of technology and the ultrafast rate of obsolescence, should the government encourage the expansion of the national laboratories? I have been working recently in Germany and have participated in a number of transnational Pan-European research projects, in which many companies and universities form a strategic team. These activities have already shown substantial results. I am also very impressed by the programs of research at the Max Planck Institute. Spectacular successes have been scored that resulted in at least one Nobel Prize and in the strengthening of the German semi-conductor industries. Should these European models be imitated?"

The West Indian economist responds.

"Madam, your examples of success in Europe and specifically in Germany are good illustrations of the vicissitudes of fortune amid the cultural backgrounds in different countries. They demonstrate the importance of understanding the all-embracing nature of the technology and its impact on society. Forgive me for using a sexist analogy. Women are fickle, as we men often say; 'La Donna est Mobile' is one of my favorite tunes, and technology is likewise mobile. It is the upbringing that counts. What I am referring to is this: Technology transfer is multifaceted and the process is likely to be more successful if the methods adopted reflect the understanding of the relevant backgrounds of the time, the place and the people involved.

"As far as I am concerned, there is no magic formula. In the United States of America the free market forces are strong. The Government has some specialization laboratories, but chooses to encourage transferrable technology by providing competitive funding from such organizations as the National Science Foundation (NSF) and the National Institute of Health. The latter is a national laboratory as well as a funding agency. This scheme has worked well and is being adjusted to reflect the need to push strategic alliances. NSF is encouraging the formation of joint research centers at universities on multidisciplinary projects involving several departments of the university and industrial partners. America has produced the largest number of Nobel Laureates and has spearheaded many technological advances and innovative applications. The test is forthcoming. Can America maintain her dwindling lead by tuning up her technology-transfer processes? Maybe one of my fellow panelists can continue with other responses to your question."

Dr. Knowall takes up this invitation.

"I agree with our friend from the West Indies entirely. Strategic alliance to me is not a myth. It is probably a term concocted by Business-School professors and it is too honeyed and glamorous. If two companies can see eye-to-eye about a joint effort to strengthen a common technological infrastructure on which the competitiveness of their businesses depends, a strategic alliance is in the making. Their specific requirements sharpen and focus their joint effort along a direct path to support their endeavors. In this manner, their effort is likely to be highly efficient. In our age of abundance, the greatest achievement lies in discovering ways to eliminate the non-essentials. Strategic alliance definitely helps.

"I'd like to add my comments on the role of the national laboratories. Big physics is an area where astronomically large sums of money must be spent before anything can be done. National or multinational efforts are logical solutions. The particle accelerators are good examples. The success lies in the intense competition that exists between these centers. They all want to outdo each other. As a result, high energy physics is still advancing. Without competition, national laboratories can be white elephants. They could easily become rest-cure accommodations for self-claimed inventors. Or they could be respected research ivory towers, dignified, secluded, isolated with nothing coming out of them. I guess I am trying to make a point for designing technology transfer into all our technological efforts. Our vigilance regarding the process of handing over the fruit of our labor is the key that helps us to make notable advances."

The Chairman looks expectantly at the audience while at the same time he senses the appropriateness of stopping the discussion with the last remark of Dr. Knowall. He seizes the temporary lull and declares.

"We can keep this discussion going indefinitely. Technology transfer, as presented by the panelists and enhanced by the questions from the audience, is a very rich and fertile area for generating debates. It is more than that. It is a thoughtful area. Our world village is getting to be a world metropolis. Everything is more abundant, including the interactions and the intersections of many of our endeavors. It is an opportune time. As Shakespeare said, 'There is a tide in the affairs of men, which, taken at the flood, leads on to fortune; omitted, all the voyage of their life is bound in shallows and in miseries.' May I take this opportunity to thank my panelists and the audience for a successful and fulfilling session."

Chapter 10

Market and Product Creation: A New Product Cycle

"Our aim is to capture 18% of the market," pronounced a marketeer. "We'll hit the market hard for the next six months and come out ahead," mused another. "Let us prepare the market carefully but be there first," strategized the marketing director.

"My friends, which products are we talking about?" the CEO commented. "Surely the methods of marketing prescribed by yourselves are valid but, in all probability, each solution is more suited to a particular product and besides, if they are applied without realism, they are just hot air.

"We have four distinct types of products, and we must make different market/product plans for each type. Hence, we will have four separate planning sessions. The first will be for our mature products for mature markets. The second will be for our new products to be sold in mature markets. Then we will discuss our new products which are designed for yet-to-be-determined markets. Finally, we will make plans for those products which are timed for a transient window of opportunity. Please be prepared to identify customer needs, ranking in priority the customers' disposable incomes, the product features and cycle, and the competitive positions."

At the first of the four planning sessions, the Director of Marketing for Mature Products stated, "25% of our products are for the mature market. We know our customers' needs. We have our customer base. We have our distribution and sales channels and service back-up. Our aim is to maintain this position and increase our profitability. This is our bread-and-butter line; we must generate the cash to build up our new businesses which take a lot of time and resources.

"Our marketing effort consists of probing the customers' needs and listening carefully to what they say about the improvements they would like. These reflect the real expectations together with the rose-tinted spectacles views which they have formed through our competitors' marketing efforts. We also try to feed our customers our product improvement plans. We give them improvements of real value and we add features which enhance their future options of using new equipment based on new concepts rather than continuously improving our current products. We try to show our customers explicitly the life-time cost of staying with the existing but improved products.

"This strategy allows us to make minimum investments in R&D and facilitates our product cost reduction through increased total production volume with well-tested production experience.

"We also try to manage the termination of a product. If a product is made obsolete or is likely to become obsolescent in the near future, we either drop the product and make every effort to guide the customer elsewhere, or we restructure the business to a smaller volume, longer delivery, higher price product for the end market. Our R&D and engineering people have always been very helpful. They are very effective in alerting us to the imminent obsolescence of a product, particularly when they have plans for a new product.

"Our strategy with mature products is to increase profitability rather than trying to increase market share. In a stable market situation, the cost of increasing market share is high. In fact, with the elimination of obsolete businesses, we are actually shrinking. This is acceptable to us since it fits our total company strategy which calls for the rise and fall of separate products. I have no problem with that, particularly as my performance is measured against the ROI of my area, while my sales volume is an agreed figure established on a company-wide basis, taking all other products into account.

"I believe in our strategy. It seems relatively standard and conservative, but it fits the new technology environment. The stable products have well-identified needs. Unless something drastic happens, the need does not suddenly vanish. Competition is on price, delivery and service. Novel features are good selling points, but the features must be significant and price increases minimal; otherwise the advantages are insufficient for the product to make a significant inroad into the market. If new technology can cause a significant reduction in cost of the product while still providing the same functions, we must adopt it or else stop making the product. This technology threat is real and important. We keep asking our R&D people to advise us. We keep estimating the costs/benefits of adopting the new technology. We support R&D projects to assess the impacts of technology on our products and we work closely with our R&D center.

"We conduct some R&D for making improvements based on our knowledge of what the customer needs. However, we devote the bulk of our R&D to cost reduction through improving yields, using new materials, simplifying the testing, etc."

The R&D manager concurred, "Maintenance of mature products is important to us. The little investment we make in R&D towards that is yielding a much higher sales/R&D ratio and a better ROI. However, the mature products are vulnerable. One day they can be wiped out suddenly through technology advances. Just look how the electronic quartz-controlled watch affected the mechanical watches. We keep a sharp eye on new technologies which could help our mature products and we keep showing possibilities to the product managers. After all, these products are earning a large portion of our profits."

The director of product development, whose responsibility it is to shift products into the correct categories, said, "This year, we are shifting fifteen products into the mature-product category since the technology impact on these products has reached a low level. This will increase the percentage of mature products by 2% to 27%. In addition, we expect to phase out three products which only accounts for 0.5% of the sales volume. I believe this is a healthy situation. In this technology-dominated age, 27% mature products is an excellent base."

The CEO said, "Let me summarize our position,

- Our mature products for the mature market are those with a good chance of having at least another three years of anticipated life.
- We continuously review our portfolio, and we eliminate those whose remaining lives are seen to be less than three years. A suitable phase-out plan will be made for each of these products.
- We continuously add to this portfolio products which are only marginally affected by technological advances.
- We use 2% of our total sales of these products on R&D to maintain their competitiveness.
- We do not vigorously attempt to increase our market shares of these products, and we make only the minimum capital investments to support them.
- We apply our greatest effort towards maximizing profit.
- The uneven distribution of mature products among our manufacturing divisions unfortunately is difficult to avoid. Our development of new products should take this situation into consideration."

The second planning session dealt with the company's new products for mature markets. The CEO opened the session with the following comments: "This is a very challenging area for us because the competition is severe and investment requirements are large.

Furthermore, nearly 50% of our products are in this category. Hence, a considerable portion of our R&D effort has been directed towards the development of these new products. We will now hear from the director of marketing for products in this category."

The marketing director of new products for mature markets rose to make his presentation.

"We faced many difficult problems in the last few years due to our imprecise recognition of the effect of technology on our products. We have several major lines of products whose future is greatly threatened by new products which are lower in cost and higher in performance. We made decisions several years ago to develop a major product line based on very advanced technology which was estimated to be ready around this year. This product line is ready for the market, but our development cost has been extremely high. We also decided during the last few years to make new products to replace many of those in our threatened product lines. Our R&D lab made an all-out assault on a broad technology front with the aim of establishing a solid base of knowledge, as well as providing the in-depth understanding needed about the potential of these technologies. At the same time the value of a good high-tech image was also considered important both for marketing as well as for recruiting purposes. On hindsight, what was not understood was the extent of the impact of technology on business. We underestimated the effort and resources needed to put technology into our businesses. We were totally unprepared to make numerous operational changes in the management and conduct of our business.

"We now realize that:

- A product can be improved in numerous ways with the use of more appropriate technologies, old and new, which are at our disposal.
- The customer-base changes when a product is improved. Usually the product is really a new product which appeals to a broader cross-section of customers. However, with certain

specific improved features, fewer customers will have the feeling that the product exactly suits their needs.

- An idealized product upgrade usually calls for the development
  of technologies which are over and above those available.
- New technology takes time and effort to mature into a form
  which is useful for product application.
- New technologies suggest new product concepts but much
  effort is involved to turn these concepts into practice.

"We were faced with a proliferation of new products which were
marginally improved versions of our old products attempting to
compete in the changing market. Our products were designed and
manufactured with our traditional procedures. We also used the same
marketing procedures. As a result, we saw a rapid escalation of costs
for our new products. The new products, at the same time, faced
rapid obsolescence.

"Fortunately, this situation is widespread through our industry.
We are by no means unique, and we have managed to struggle along.
This year we propose to make some major changes. These changes
are timely since we are more prepared for them. Our Central
Laboratory has exposed us to many future possibilities. We have also
had serious difficulties in our business units in incorporating such
possibilities into our products. Both sides have sobered up. We are
now in a position to make the Central Lab responsive to the realistic requirements which emerge from our product decisions. These
decisions in turn are now guided by a more realistic understanding
and assessment of our business aspirations and market possibilities in
the light of our available resources.

"We have taken the following actions:

- We are expanding our marketing efforts by concentrating on
  fewer improved products and by organizing a technical service
  and an educational support area, utilizing people from our
  technical areas to help in consolidating the perception of our
  targeted customers in selected sectors of our customer-base.

This is in recognition that improved products are really new products in a highly competitive environment.

- We require the product improvement to be time-phased and applicable partially or wholly to several products. This is to combat the problem of a long development time and a short product life. We are in the position to do this, thanks to our in-depth knowledge of technology trends and our experience in technology insertion. We can estimate with reasonable reliability the impact of technology on the performance of the product over a time period long enough to make cost recovery possible. At the same time, we are instituting new manufacturing procedures to help in the same way.

- We use new technologies on short-term tasks only when it is absolutely necessary, but we will not hesitate to consider the use of appropriate technologies, new and old, in order to achieve our product features on a planned schedule. In those cases, realistic assessments of the effort needed and its timeliness are made and actions are initiated towards meeting the schedule.

- We urge our Central Laboratory to concentrate on a few enabling technologies with the highest impact on our current and planned endeavors and to help us establish a means to obtain other enabling technologies externally.

- We recommend an investment of 10% of total sales of products in this category on R&D efforts relating to these products.

"I suppose what we are doing reflects our recognition that in an environment of unlimited opportunities, we must make our choices match our aspirations and, particularly, our resources. We cannot afford to do everything."

The CEO then commented, "I am pleased with your realism, but I am concerned about our ability to meet our growth target. Furthermore, the marketing cost per product appears to increase while the volume of products sold appears to decrease. This will make the product too costly. Where are we deriving the cost savings?"

"Synergism is probably the best word to describe where we make savings," the marketing director said confidently. "Let me explain further:

"Recently, many of our competitors and we ourselves have said that we are total system suppliers. If you buy from us, we can sell you an entire system or parts of a system or even a separate piece of equipment. Even our separate items of equipment can function on their own and still be compatible with our system. Our attempt is to build synergism into our sales effort. This could, in an ideal situation, spread our marketing costs over a large array of products.

"However, this is seldom a real situation. What we are doing is to pay more than lip service to synergism. We try our best to plan groups of products which will have technical synergism and target them towards customer groups requiring this synergism. We also do our planning iteratively, repeatedly back and forth. This means that we start either with customer needs and derive products, or we begin with products and derive customer needs. All the time, we make sure that we get synergism and the opportunity to share resources. We must derive savings somewhere.

"Let me use our traditional memory typewriter product as an illustration. This product was intended for the office market where there is an urgent need to improve secretarial efficiency. For example, a lawyer's office has to prepare many individual documents which have relatively minor differences, and a memory typewriter saves considerable time and effort. We moved into this business not as a natural extension of manual and electric typewriters, but as a result of technological innovation. We had a telex operation with keyboard and electronic circuit capabilities. The combination of the keyboard and the availability of simple microprocessors and electronic memory chips allowed us to introduce a memory typewriter relatively quickly. For a while the market for our typewriters was good, particularly when we improved the type print quality and output speed with our improved printing mechanisms.

"Now we are considering dropping this product line since memory typewriters have virtually been wiped out by the word-processors and other products associated with personal computers. In our product planning sessions last year, we looked at this product long and hard. We reasoned that we are in the telex business and the memory typewriter business. Both are threatened with extinction soon, despite many technological innovations. We observed:

- The keyboard is common;
- The memory and control can easily be implemented with current technology so that the product will achieve higher performance with little added cost;
- The output printer is obsolete, but faster and newer versions are available;
- The customer-base still exists in many offices, but they are enamoured with the computer-based systems.

"Our options are:

- To fit our memory typewriter to a smaller market where it can serve as a low-cost limited-capability word-processor to compete with the upper end of the simple typewriter market.
- To make the sub-units available to personal computer, word-processor, and workstation makers as matching components.
- To use the sub-units as a line of new products for office applications.

"The last option is by no means simple to undertake. We would have a strong advantage only if the sub-units are both price- and performance-competitive.

"We made a two-prong decision. On the one hand, the sub-units are to be made attractive for the original equipment market (OEM). We are able to take this step since our products are compatible with other commonly used keyboards/printers and are price-competitive. On the other hand, the sub-units are to be considered for our new memory typewriter product which is designed as an adjunct to more powerful word-processors or personal computers. The advantage is to allow simple jobs to be done on an easier-to-use machine while permitting documents to be reloaded in the word-processor for extensive editing wherever necessary.

"Both these steps can be taken with investments in marketing and engineering, recoverable from the extended life of the product over the next three years. At the same time, the upgraded printer and memory are valuable for other products for the office which we are planning."

But the CEO was not entirely satisfied, and he asked, "Are we still burying our head in the sand, since our presence in the office equipment market is really very small? The memory typewriter and telex belong to the by-gone offices."

"I believe we have a claim to that market even though we are not in the mainstream. We are there with a product, and we have an established entry and link with the customers, even though we are on the sideline. We stand a chance to enlarge our presence, especially since our sub-units are basic parts of man-machine interfaces. What we have is a strategy of elongating the life of our current product, keeping access to the customer open, and trying to make our sub-units into building blocks for future systems. It is a sound approach even without the future promises," retorted the marketing director.

At this point the director of marketing for new products in new markets entered the discussion. "As I see it, the justification for introducing a new product into a new market must be based on strength derived from previous experience. In addition, our future growth is strongly dependent on new products in new markets. I believe we have several good sub-units in the memory typewriter which we could use in new product developments."

"Thank you for your support," continued the director of new products in mature markets, "The major difference between you and me is the fact that you have to spend even more effort in creating the new markets. In this case of the memory typewriter, I am treading dangerously near to creating a new market too. I would like to conclude by saying that on most of my products we try to group the products and customers carefully and make joint improvements and interchangeable parts in order to derive synergism."

"Good work," commented the CEO. "I feel in my guts that we need to be very vigilant and wise. This is a very challenging area. Let me try to give a short summary of this complex area.

- A product which can be greatly impacted by technology in a mature market appears, when improved, as a new product and must be treated accordingly.
- Marketing and technology commonality are needed between a number of related products to generate sufficient synergism to reduce the investment per product.
- A short product development time for the initial version of the product followed by a planned upgrading helps to elongate the life span of the product (through a broad appreciation of technology trends).
- Just as for new products for new markets, targeted customers must be guided into making their decisions for our products."

The CEO began the planning session on new products for new markets as follows: "In our environment of many opportunities, the customers are facing the impossible situation of making good choices from an infinity of alternatives. This is really the reason why new products in a mature market are so difficult. The partial knowledge the customers have, in fact generates pre-bias and gives rise to unrealistic requirements. We have to overcome the pre-bias before we can show rationally the advantages of our new products in the mature market. However, for a new product with no market, we can start from ground zero. We identify for the would-be customers the need which is real but latent and then the unique market is there for our unique product. This is a leadership situation where we must build the momentum and then run the race till we touch the tape first. The growth of companies along this course is risky but less exhausting than trying to keep their position in the mature market with the large number of new products that are sensitive to technological impacts. It should be undertaken judiciously."

The marketing director for new products for new markets smiled broadly and said, "Our CEO has done my selling job already. I can launch straight into what we are doing in this area. We are planning to establish a 15% share of this company's total business with new products for which we need to create the new markets.

"The basic criteria for selecting new products are based on our

- strength in the relevant enabling technologies,
- knowledge gained from our long-range R&D projects,
- entrepreneurial talents,

matched to the perceived needs of would-be customers which are emerging due to our changing social and economic environment. Since improvements in information handling in the work environment are urgently needed by all types of organizations, our new products are in this area.

"From our experience of successes and failures so far, we place strong emphasis on having an adequate support infrastructure in place before we launch any new product. In other words, when we introduce a unique new product in a unique new market place, we make sure that the support system for that market is actually in place at the time of introduction of the product. For example, if we introduce a location indicator for an automobile at a time when only a few cities are providing the location data, this product is likely to fail. On the other hand, when personal computers were introduced with rudimentary software and no networking possibilities, their success were initially phenomenal. The infrastructure was not considered incomplete. The explanation is probably this. The personal computer was introduced as an affordable computer for an individual. It conjured up the image that the individual could now have this powerful tool which would give him the ability to do what he previously knew could only be done by a big company. It also had the image of being an extended hand calculator which made arithmetic so much easier.

These factors constituted a sufficient inducement for many to buy the personal computer, even though few derived real and full benefits from it. Nevertheless, the continuing success of the personal computer depends largely on building up the infrastructure to allow customers to derive more of the benefits for which they really bought the machine. Consequently, the sales of personal computers will rise when networking and software are in place for these machines to be used effectively in offices. Eventually, home users will have the support system to make personal computers indispensable in our daily life instead of gathering dust in a corner.

"Our Central Research Lab has been working on a basic research project which permits an overall view of technology trends and generates new ideas for future possibilities. It has also several other projects which are the basis of probable new products and which allow an orderly development of our strength in enabling technologies. From this rich store we select a few each year and start feasibility studies towards making them the basis of new products for our identified, but yet to be created, markets. After a year or two, business objectives are formed and market creation activity, along with product development, is initiated. During the analysis and planning phases, target markets for each product are determined, the scope of each project is set, and the required investments for each product are estimated. We attempt to seek the minimum market size compatible with available resources. We analyze whether the infrastructure is sufficiently complete. When the ROI is estimated to be acceptable, the product is launched with full speed and deliberation until completion. The marketing effort is to ensure that when the product is available, the market will actually be there. The actual development time is kept very short, just as in our new projects for the mature market. We use our strengths of having total market control and an appropriate internal technical base work for us. We supplement these efforts by using the existing external infrastructure, both in technical and market support, to really drive home our advantages.

"Our CEO has consistently backed us in our internal

entrepreneurial endeavors. He has allocated resources but left out the normal controls to allow unimpeded progress of the work over the entire agreed period of the project. It is, as it were, a gamble with finite risks. This turns out to be probably the most significant reason for our success in our first attempt. Three years ago, we agreed on a three-year project to develop a special computer especially designed to work efficiently with a computer language used by people working in the artificial intelligence area. This machine was planned, designed and pre-marketed. The development of the machine started about a year ago, using available technology. The sales this year are as planned, right on schedule. We now know of a competitor looming over the horizon. We are not worried; in fact, we fully anticipated that. In two years, we will have moved to a different part of this market. We are looking at that seriously at this moment. The computer for artificial intelligence was deliberately planned with only a three-year life; it derives its synergy from the use of only off-the-shelf components. We treat the computers for artificial intelligence as a series of new machines, and we plan to sell them as new products into new markets each time.

"Our investment return is targeted for three years. The entire investment package is treated differently from those of our products in other areas. Here we make a large initial investment both in development and capital and we aim for a quick return of the investment with profits. The short time constant for investment return is not common for an equipment manufacturer but it is a meaningful experiment. As we gather more experience, we will consider longer time constants for the investment return."

"If this continues to develop along the lines you have just outlined, will we ever have any stable products?" the CEO enquired. "Maybe this is the future trend in products sensitive to technology changes. I am sure we will have a certain percentage of longer-run products reflecting some of our customers' continuing needs. This situation is common in some industries; for example, a Broadway play is a one-off product designed to achieve very fast returns, usually in less than a year. Another example is a broadcasting TV program. It is produced with a specific audience in mind and its value is spent after only one showing. Incidentally, the targeting of the specific audience must, therefore, be very precisely done."

"So," the CEO continued, "this reminds me that I need to look at the structure of the company. As we get more and more involved in new businesses, we will need a mobile-line management force and low-capitalized bases so that we can switch to different products easily.

"Our staff function will be more geared to provide administrative services rather than project management and control. The overall planning function must serve as a consultancy to provide facts and figures relating to a broad range of business areas. They could give advice on the overall business direction of the company and guide the units to select their targets so that synergy exists throughout the company. In fact, the staff function probably could be provided by the line people in a dual role. The important thing is to make the system flexible, non-permanent, but with continuity.

"We have to understand what we mean by proprietary information. As I see it, our competitiveness is dependent on how effectively we can make use of technology to produce a needed product. Our technical solution is one of many possibilities. The chance of finding some equally good alternative is really there. It is better to share knowledge with others and not keeping it proprietary. This serves two important functions:

- By confiding in others, particularly our peers, they may share our enthusiasm and adopt our solution to their products. In other words, we are getting the needed publicity through our peers. Our customers will readily be convinced that the approach we take is good and trustworthy, since our competitors are also touting the same virtues. We have created an effective bandwagon.
- By sharing with others, our adopted technology areas may be

developed further through the joint efforts. The infrastructure supporting our product could become even more complete.

"If we remember that ours is a leadership strategy, then we should share all our proprietary information.

"Again let me try to summarize:

- New products and new markets must be created together.
- In the first round, the product should have a short return on investment cycle. The total commitment in resource and time is to be assured and agreed from the start.
- These products should be selected from a list prepared by the Central Research Laboratory.
- Although vertical integration of the new product is desirable, the company unit aspiring to spearhead the product need only to do the orchestration from a few internal vantage points. The mode of operation is interdependent rather than independent."

The CEO then stated, "We have reviewed these product areas and have enunciated our policy guidelines in each. I propose that, rather than having a fourth planning session, we discuss the products which are designed and timed for a transient window of opportunity now. Our discussion can be brief because we only occasionally have such a product. Every now and then an opportunity arises in such a way that business can be conducted advantageously for a particular company which happens to realize this opportunity is within its grasp.

"For example, a toy company sees the opportunity to introduce microprocessors to a range of its products. Suddenly, it realizes that they could introduce a gimmicky toy computer. They could be lured into thinking that they have now entered the big league of computer suppliers. Nonetheless, the toy computer is a good opportunity even though it is a transient product.

"We may regard a transient product as one which can brought into being by the chance convergence of all appropriate resources in a company. Even if the product should be outside its normal business area, it may have the advantage of being available at a time when its need is perceived."

The CEO concluded, "Today we have taken an important step in the right direction. We have laid down our guidelines on how we conduct our business in these separate product areas. We can see the need to make deliberate and well-coordinated changes in many areas. Thank you, ladies and gentlemen. I am now closing this meeting with one further action item. I would like the Manufacturing Director to organize a discussion on how we should design and produce products with short life cycles."

At the special meeting, the directors of manufacturing, engineering, purchasing, quality control and marketing were all present.

The Manufacturing Director stated, "Even without the short life cycles of products, we at manufacturing are facing enormous change. We are dealing with complex parts and more precise assembly. We face complex test requirements. In some cases, we are dealing with new fabrication technologies which require clean areas, strict environmental control and dangerous chemicals. All these are leading to high capital costs to set up a manufacturing area. In addition, we now have to cope with short product runs associated with short product cycles. I am overwhelmed by the enormity of the problem. I must say I welcome this occasion to see what we can do jointly."

The Engineering Director declared emphatically, "In the engineering area, I have been urging my engineers to identify functional building blocks whenever a specific product is under development. I believe that if we have a good collection of these, we can design many products by using a combination of these standard building blocks. This approach actually imposes constraints on the design approach and can lead to less cost effective products. However, taken as a whole, the cost savings can be significant. Besides, testing and parts qualification can be more rational. Still, one of my major problems is the need of one or more key advanced devices just available on the market, or sometimes only as prototype samples for each new product. These are usually the components and parts which enable the new product to meet the performance and cost targets. Every one of these devices has probably only one reliable supplier, and qualification is not too meaningful since exhaustive testing cannot be completed in a timely manner.

"Another major problem is to document the equipment for manufacturing. This process is lengthy and is standing in our way as a big bottleneck, preventing the quick turnaround of the product."

The Quality Control Director echoed the same sentiments: "Our quality assurance method is undermined by the large number of new devices and circuit boards needing qualification. We cannot even keep up with the growth of standard parts lists and vendor qualifications. We are forced to use preventive maintenance to meet our reliability commitment, since we have no meaningful accelerated aging data."

The Purchasing Director simply said, "My old problem of negotiating for best large-volume prices is replaced by the problem of finding vendors who will commit to our specifications and who have some credibility."

The Marketing Director rejoined, "Our problem can be solved by using fewer not-yet-qualified components. We must design fewer new products involving new untried components and increase our research activity to include the means to indirectly test for reliability. We must work more closely with component suppliers and stress the need for mutual survival." The Marketing Director then summarized his recommendations:

- When new products with a short life cycle are the order of the day, the search for product commonality and good working relationships with critical parts suppliers are mandatory.
- Marketing directors should be urged to work closely with engineering so that the products have planned improvements and provide progressively more features, but restrict these products to those which satisfy the planned requirements of the market.
- Engineering, manufacturing, quality control and purchasing

must work closely to build up the production unit cohesively. The aim is to shorten the development time and the production time through accumulating reinforcing experiences.

At a quiet moment, the CEO reflects upon the meaning of the new product cycle. He is jotting down his thoughts on two sheets of paper. On one, he lists the impact of technology on marketing; on the other, he lists his planned actions.

List 1—Impact of Technology on Marketing

- A product can be launched when marketing action has created specific customers' need(s).
- Interdependence between supplier and customer results in a broader acceptance and minimizes resource expenditure. It is a preferred operational mode.
- Focusing and targeting a given product to specific customer needs are essential and are to be done in keeping with available resources.
- Integrated engineering and marketing actions are essential in getting a product to the market in minimum time.
- Synergy is marketing and engineering actions is needed to overcome the effects of small market sizes for specific products.
- A midcourse change almost always requires an expensive use of resources because it is equivalent to starting everything again.

List 2—Planned Actions

- Create a working database for aiding the business decision-making process. The CEO and the marketing, engineering and manufacturing directors are jointly responsible for the internal consistency of this database. The responsibility for upgrading is to reside for three months with each person in turn in the order listed above, beginning with every annual planning cycle.
- Initiate and continue actions on interdependence at all levels

of operations internally and externally. Balance risks and advantages against resource expenditure. Encourage both friendly and competitive ties.

- Regard research and advanced development as a part of our marketing tools. Hence, all R&D activities have business objectives and should contain actions to let would-be customers and partners know of their purpose and value. Long-term activities are equally important and effective as marketing tools.
- Increase synergism by requiring that products be designed from a limited range of appropriate functional blocks.
- Increase synergism by identifying the customer groups within which we are to target different customer-bases for our products.
- Avoid the temptation of apparent greener pastures. They only look greener through our envy, generated by our inability to get there.
- Consider unbiased service consultation and advice to customers as essential elements in the conduct of business.
- Set up consultancies or promote consultations for customers and would-be customers to help them to identify their needs and to use these needs as feedback channels for identifying and consolidation of planned future products.

All this because technology has increased our options. What a fascinating challenge!

Chapter 11

The Third World

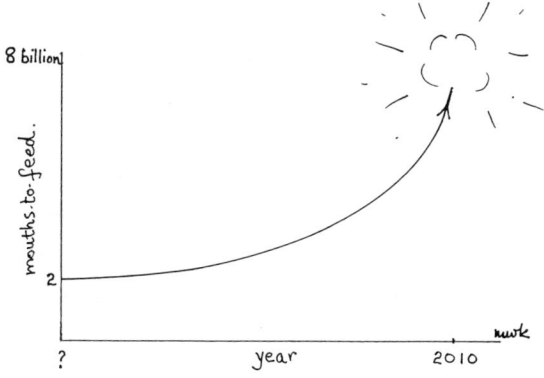

Within the global village, many well-guarded oases have been created and occupied by the lucky and the enterprising. Outside of these are the hardier areas. Where habitation is possible, swarms of the less fortunate and the less privileged scrape together a mere existence. Some parts are still fertile land which were undoubtedly oases in their times. Overpopulation and poor organization have created a situation of overdemand for the products from the land. War and natural disasters have not helped. These are areas struggling to arrest the decline against overwhelming odds. These are the areas trying to play a catch-up game with scarce effective means. These are the Third World.

To the people of the Third World the consequence of abundance created by technology is that of apparent hopelessness. The prognosis is extremely poor. With a productivity per capita some hundred times higher than the corresponding one of the poor, the rich grow richer; the poor have to grow at a much higher rate just not to get poorer. If the poor borrow from the rich in order to buy in the needed technologies for faster growth, the situation is worsened. They end up having to pay all their growth to the rich in interest payments.

Every day the people in the Third World struggle to survive. They appear to have no choice. They rise at dawn and retire as night falls. In between, they toil at manual labor if they are lucky enough to find work, or they simply mope the day away worrying about the next bowl of food. There is no time for leisure. On rare occasions they may make their way on a dusty and bumpy road, on a rickety overfilled bus, to the overwhelmingly crowded city. They swim around in the human sea and surface sometimes to gawk at the fine displays in the shops. There are plenty of imported goods at prices well beyond their reach. These commodities are for the local well-to-do people. In any case what is the use of a refrigerator where there is no electricity, and what can be viewed on a television set without power? Still it is not a crime to dream about possessing such luxuries, even in the Third World.

The basic common problem is caused by having too many mouths to feed given the state of development of the countries. The situation is aggravated by the shrinkage of the world into a global village as a result of technological advances. Through books, photographs, television programs, movies and many other forms of information media, through the opportunities to travel to distant lands, the temptation to indulge in luxurious life styles reaches almost everywhere to breed discontent and unrealistic aspirations. Can technology help to redress this human tragedy? To construct a balanced and useful answer to this question, we should understand many related issues.

There are the population issues; the aged, birth control, work ethics, and self-esteem are all integral to this problem. There are other major issues of no less importance: political systems, resource limits and pollution. Political systems generate knotty issues of sovereignty, democracy, order and military might. Resource limits include lack of power sources, consumables, food production, etc. Pollution is a global issue. Technology-related pollution is an especially difficult topic. With all these issues, the technology impact on the Third World can be seen to be complex.

The population issue is a very serious one. The rate of birth is at least 2% per annum in the area where nearly 70% of the world's population reside. At the same time, the life expectancy of human beings is lengthening rapidly. As a result the number of mouths to feed is increasing at a rate that will double the world population in about the year 2010. On the assumption, unfortunately untrue, that everybody is presently self-sufficient, production of everything must be doubled in the same time frame. This would generate enormous pressure on the prevailing production machinery already creaking under the current load. Productivity improvement through the introduction of better techniques, especially better management backed by the development of a support infrastructure, is mandatory.

Looking at this issue in greater detail, we can see much of the complex interrelated problems. In China, for instance, improvement in medical care has led to a growth of the aged population. The longevity of life slows the rate of decrease of the population. With the parents living longer but physically less able, the living space is under pressure. The rarity in the past of having four generations living together now becomes commonplace. More have to share the same space. Besides overcrowding, tradition deals another blow to the family. For as long as the elders are alive they are regarded as wise and to be venerated. Their feeble and conservative minds often run counter to needed progress. The provision of added medical care becomes a drain on national resources whether it is provided by the family or by the scarce medical infrastructure of the countryside.

Traditionally, rural parents want as many children as possible, especially male offsprings, since they represent additional labor to work on the farm. They are also insurance for old age on whom the parents can count on for support and care. The parents would not see the problem of overpopulation, since within their own lifetime the increased mouths could be fed on the increased productivity from the farm, especially if they happen to farm on fertile lands. Traditions die hard. This desire to have more children permeates throughout China, often leading to lower standards of living as population out-strips productivity.

Throughout the Third World, as a result of male dominance, births are regarded as natural events which God or Deity has or-dained and with which no human being must interfere. Moreover, children are the hope of the future; they are a blessing since they unite the family, are extra work-hands for the household and will be the companions and caretakers of their parents in old age. In any case, apart from celibacy or infanticide, fertile couples go forth and multiply. Whenever governments try to introduce birth controls, the response from the majority in a biased world of sex inequality is one of disbelief. India tried the intra-uterus contraception devices and voluntary sterilization with only marginal success. The former method is hazardous to health and the latter is expensive and psychologically hard for men to accept. China is trying the one-child rule coupled with incentives and punishments. The rule is somewhat ignored in the countryside. Indoctrination coupled with education on birth control, and the popularization of easy-to-use contraceptives have so far reduce the birth rate to a little below 2%. In other areas around the world the rate stays at 4% annually.

The rate of population growth had never been a problem. It was relatively low in the days of high infant mortality and low average life expectancy. The population density in every region was low enough to be comfortably supported by the produce from the land even with primitive farming techniques. As this growth is insidiously maintained over the years and the counterbalances all but gone, there comes a time when the exponential growth takes off with a vengeance. After so many centuries our human population in the immediate past fifty years has doubled twice from less than one billion to more than four billion. Suddenly the produce from the land using largely traditional methods cannot meet the demand. Traditional beliefs must be re-vised. We must control the rate of growth of our population and increase the productivity. The social structure has been fundamentally altered.

Fortunately, in the global village, territorial disputes are not major contentions anymore. The days of empire building are long past. Most nations are reconciled to the fact that, for richer or for poorer, they are to improve their wealth within their allotted land. Their mutual survivals are interrelated in a tangled web of intersecting actions. The rich must help the poor to be less poor in order to avoid the possible development of an extreme situation, in which a few percent of the world population gorge while the majority starve—a highly explosive situation.

Nations have roots and they cannot easily adopt alien culture without understanding whether it can flourish when grafted on to its own roots. The United States of America has a short history of just over 200 years. The founding fathers were adventurers and pioneers. They migrated from old worlds to seek a new life. They believed in hard work, the sanctity of life and the rights of the individual. Successive groups of immigrants are of the same genre. After being initially discriminated against and exploited, they eventually merged as part of the whole nationhood. It is easy to appreciate the words used in their "Declaration of Independence." With little historic baggage to carry, the U.S.A. emerged from its early isolationism to be the dominant power with the wealth and the military might to substantiate their claim on the world stage.

China is one of the ancient countries where civilization was born. Around 4,000 years ago the social relationships had already reached a high degree of sophistication. Over its long history China has evolved a governmental system and civic customs to ensure order and stability. Up to this century, each dynasty lasted for several hundred years. Some were dynasties of the barbaric invaders of the Central Kingdom. These were said to be "Chinesified"; they adopted a finely honed system of order and stability. Within this system, the government is despotic but is seen as benevolent and is there to maintain order. The people are free so long as they cause no troubles, or in other words, they remain subservient. Every few hundred years a dynasty collapsed, usually due to a weak leader who could not resist the temptations of corruption fueled so readily by absolute power. Unfortunately, a system designed for super stability suppresses change and innovation. China, after attaining peak power and cultural eminence some 600 years ago, has been declining ever since.

Japan could have had the same fate. The Meiji reform was the critical turning point. It showed that the strength of the stable dynastic system, if it is used wisely by able and enlightened leaders, can painlessly and effectively introduce reforms. The timing happened to be good as the Meiji reforms occurred in the days when the European might was not yet overwhelming and Russia was the least prepared. The victory of the Russo-Japanese war boosted the confidence of the Japanese people. Thus, in a controlled manner Japan marched towards modernization. Contrasting with the later event of the Opium War between England and China, the difference was in the tardiness of China to modernize and the growing strength of the European powers influenced by the Industrial Revolution. The postwar Japan took on Western methods and added to them the traditional disciplinary approaches. Even if this is not the sole reason, it is an important contribution to the rise of Japan to the rank of number one in the world for productivity per capita.

The natives of the United Kingdom had resisted Roman invaders. They were a tough lot. As an island state, survival through changes was widely accepted. Throughout the development of Europe, the United Kingdom fought to exert its dominance and its right to be a sovereign state. Her seafaring exploits brought her added resources and wealth and at one time her Kingdom and Dominions circumscribed the world. After World War II, the Empire disintegrated in the wake of the winds of independence. The retrenchment was as traumatic as the fall of the Central Kingdom had been in China. With a history of change as her experience base, the United Kingdom proved to be much more resilient. Over time, the United Kingdom adjusted to a reduced but nevertheless important role as one of the leading industrialized nations of the West.

Mexico, like the United States of America, is a relatively new nation, built by old-world emigrants principally from Spain and Portugal. Tobacco and coffee kept the Mexican economy afloat. When the OPEC oil cartel recently held the world to ransom with a huge increase in the price of oil, the discovery of this valuable commodity in the Gulf of Mexico made possible the dream of becoming a leading oil-rich country. Mexicans aspired to live as one of the wealthiest countries in the world. The banks of the world agreed to lend huge sums of money to Mexico for major development projects. Sadly, the oil bubble burst when the cartel fell apart, leaving Mexico with a huge debt and deposits of oil which were not economical to extract for a market paying the restored pre-crisis prices.

The Wealth of Nations by Adam Smith and *Das Kapital* by Karl Marx are tomes for theoretical presentations only. The social and political development of the world, aided and abetted by technological advances, has reached a stage of coexistence and interdependence. With all the military might of the U.S.A. and Russia, the problems of Vietnam and Afghanistan were not solved. The threat of economic collapse on a global scale prevent the rich nations with all their wealth from abandoning the poor nations to fate. With the understanding of the problems in the Third World and a state of abundance created by technology, can the problems of the world be solved in such a way that the poor get richer while the rich remain rich? Can the sense of hopelessness be transformed into hopefulness?

The clue is possibly in the word, "Interdependence." At this moment, approximately 10% of the world's people are using 90% of all the resources. The rate of consumption of natural resources by these people was considered so worrisome that a series of reports were written under the aegis of the Club of Rome. The overly pessimistic reports were labeled as messages from the "gloom and doom" people. The predictions of early exhaustion of the natural resource reserves of the world, though premature, are nevertheless a reality of the future. The Club of Rome reports were helpful in slowing down consumption. Raising the growth of the economy by increasing consumption for consumption's sake has become passé. The rich nations started programs to look at resource recycling, began to research alternative primary energy production, and turned towards service-oriented economy for growth. Quality rather than quantity became the measure of achievement.

Labor-intensive production tasks are dispersed to lower labor cost areas to keep the costs of many consumer goods at a generally affordable level for more people. Participation in this process earns hard currencies for the Third World so that much needed techniques and appropriate production aids, particularly those that can improve production control, can be purchased without running up huge debts. The process of catching up can at last begin.

As the quality of life in the rich countries begins to reach a plateau, the rate of growth slows unless the rich participate through joint investment in the developing world. The developing nations can insist on a win-win situation since a competitive situation exists amongst all the rich players. One developing country may have valuable natural resources, another may have plenty of well-disciplined low cost labor, yet another may have the best geographic location for servicing trade activities. Each should capitalize on its own strength and bargain aggressively for what it needs according to its own priorities. There should be sufficient givers and takers to make a happy global village.

In this process of strategic alliances, some players may be greedy and unscrupulous. The transactions could involve arbitrary reduction of safety practices resulting in the generation of health hazards to the workers, and pollution damages to the world. Fortunately, there are the conscience-raisers: nature conservationists, antipollution activists and the like. They have raised these issues before governments and have heightened the awareness of the public. A worldwide movement now forces most governments to take effective actions. Even if life is valued somewhat differently in different parts of the world, the manufacturing of products in a hazardous environment by child labor is unacceptable in this day and age. And pollution is a global problem.

In the matter of nuclear power generation, without stringent safety precautions and proper management, such a power station is like a latent nuclear bomb waiting to go off. Nuclear power, nevertheless, is the most economical electrical power. Although it poses a risk, it will still be chosen as the preferred source of electrical power by many developing and developed nations. The responsibilities are awesome. In a melt-down the nuclear contamination would not stop at national boundaries. In the cause of writing this book we have had the Chernobyl Disaster. The full extent of its effect has not yet been all disclosed to the public.

Initially the use of DDT was hailed as the final solution against pests. It was effective and easily applied. Unfortunately, DDT remains an active chemical after it is absorbed by insects. As the dead insects were eaten by other animals, the buildup of DDT levels in the food chain accumulated, until DDT-related diseases were discovered in humans. At the same time, some insects were developing immunity to DDT. It was finally banned from agricultural usage. Sadly, surreptitious usage of DDT in underdeveloped countries is still continuing.

The cosmetic industry sells many spray-on products. With the use of freon gas, pressurized spray dispensers became very popular. The spray produced was a fine mist instead of the wimpy jet from a finger-operated air-pumped sprayer. Spray-on products multiplied exponentially worldwide. Some years later, scientists discovered a possible connection between the appearance of a hole over the South Pole in the protective ozone layer high above the earth's surface, and the increased amount of freon in the atmosphere. It was conjectured that the extent of the freon concentration had caused the ozone to be depleted from the upper atmosphere.

The next major pollution problem currently under investigation is the discharge of industrial-waste gases into the atmosphere which cause the formation of acid rain. Large areas of forest are suspected to be affected. The industrial discharges are also linked to the increase in carbon dioxide concentration in the atmosphere. The dense carbon dioxide gas stays close to the surface of the earth and traps heat in a greenhouse effect. This excess of heat can cause the melting of the polar ice. These large-scale effects are still conjectures and are not positively identified. A worldwide investigation has just begun. If proven to be true, then the problems of the Third World will be harder to solve. The extra cost of pollution controls, when added to the costs of production in the Third World, will greatly lower the competitiveness of their products and will have a crippling effect on their economy. Since the simultaneous industrialization of the developing countries would involve a massive usage of energy which would consequently generate very large amounts of pollutants, the cost of pollution controls cannot be avoided.

Being in a global village becomes a concern of all its population. All must pool their resources in an equitable way so that, with the aid of their rich neighbors, the poor can generate a progressively better deal for themselves. The concept and practice of interdependence must be clearly understood by everyone. Without technology the problems of the Third World cannot be solved. With technology there is a chance. The consequence of abundance created by technology can be hope for the Third World.

Epilogue

muurk   The Business Tree

Has business been profoundly impacted by technology? After reading through this book, the reader probably will answer in the affirmative. However, on reflection, he may say, "Damn it. I really cannot see the profound change, only a subtle alteration of emphasis." Both viewpoints are really admissible. Let us return to some of the premises put forward and largely substantiated by the concrete examples given in previous chapters.

"Perhaps the most significant factor which technology has brought to us is the means for products to be tailored to meet and satisfy individual needs at affordable prices."

"Technological progress has brought us, at this stage, a confluence of new tools which, if used properly, could create a cooperative effect with a great deal of synergism. A vast range of opportunities are waiting to be exploited."

"Technology impacts directly and indirectly on the risks and opportunities of commerce and industry."

"Our tastes and expectations are associated with our needs. These are, therefore, possible business opportunities. Our knowledge of and experience with technology are the tools helping us to imagine and realize products to meet our needs."

Clearly technology has significant impact, but the conduct of business can be viewed as a change in emphasis, a change brought about as a consequence of abundance which has resulted in unlimited but unfocused opportunities. In every business endeavor the broadened scope and widened choice demand a shift in the way resources are applied in order to limit the risks while attaining business goals.

From mature products in a mature market to new products in a new market the task of gathering and giving sufficient and relevant information is a challenging one. This is promoting a great deal of action in the information services area. The life and death of products, the competitiveness and health of industry, and the peace and prosperity of the world depend on our ability to make information work for us individually, in groups and as a whole.

The new emphasis in business is one of *attending to details while not losing sight of all the related big pictures.* This allows decisions on unique products for unique customers to be made and held to which will later result in success and profits. *A Choice Fulfilled* describes it all.

Within this book many concrete examples of business endeavors are discussed in some detail. Even though these do not correspond to actual cases, they could be happening in real life somewhere, sometime. It is important to point out that every case, real or fictitious, has a unique background and must be carefully recognized. The assessment of technology impact and the approach in the conduct of business for that particular case must be carefully tailored. This is a corollary of the theorem on infinite opportunities. Every company should have some people who can provide such assessments and advice, and they should also have external consultants with the appropriate database and incisive minds to provide unbiased views and an ability to increase the breadth of coverage. Such an investment is like a person with poor sight and hearing buying a pair of spectacles and a hearing aid. They are necessary, and they must fit.

The book *In Search of Excellence* distills from case studies the essence of good management that worked well in real practice. These case studies clearly illustrate the different sets of requirements which were needed to make each of the companies successful up to the time when the case studies were made. In the context of the arguments put forward in this book, such cases are past examples that can be used to verify the validity of this predictive model, which aims at bringing to the fore those criteria which will make future businesses successful. However, let there be a warning. When choices are infinite, solutions are also infinite. Only by hard work, guided by a sound under-standing of the purpose and aim of the business endeavor and helped by recognizing the impact and emphasis of the environment, as this book attempts to offer, will wise choices and good solutions be implemented successfully.

Glossary

anode: the part of a vacuum tube to which electrons are attracted.

Application Specific Integrated Circuit (ASIC): semi-conductor circuit designed for a specific usage.

artificial intelligence (AI): computer simulation of human intelligence.

automatic location indicators: electronic map display showing the position of the vehicle.

Band Theory: solid state theory in physics in which electronic changes in solids are depicted to exist in discrete bands of energies.

biomolecules: molecules of living materials such as cells, proteins.

cathode: the part of a vacuum tube from which electrons are emitted.

central processing unit (CPU): the part of a computer where computation takes place.

computer-aided design (CAD): design process with the helpful use of computers.

cortisone drugs: anti-inflammatory medicine.

covalent bond: a special way two atoms are joined.

crystalline material: material whose atoms are arranged in regular repeated order.

dynamic reconfiguration: a circuit configuration which can be repeatedly changed at any time.

electro-optic materials: a material whose optical characteristics can be altered by electrical field or *vice versa*.

electrode: an anode or a cathode.

electronic data-processing equipment: an electronic apparatus that manipulates electronic signals or data.

electronic mail system: a post or mail system between computers.

epitaxy: a technique of growing single crystal material in thin layers on a material substrate.

fiber optics: a hair-thin glass fiber designed for conducting light signals over long distances, just as wire for electricity.

fiber waveguide sensors: detectors of pressure, temperature, and other physical parameters made with fiber optic waveguides.

Fourier transform (transformation): a mathematical function originally suggested by the mathematician Fourier. It is used to convert a time varying signal to be represented by a set of frequencies.

gallium arsenide: a semi-conductor material particularly good for making high frequency devices and light-emitting devices.

Hall effect: It describes the flow of electric current within a conductor when placed in a magnetic field.

integrated circuit: an electronic circuit with a number of transistors and their interconnections fabricated in an integrated form on a semi-conductor wafer.

junction diode: a two-terminal semi-conductor device with a p-n junction. It works like a vacuum diode.

large-scale integration: an integrated circuit with thousands of transistors on a single wafer.

laser optical discs: a disc with usually digital data written on it and can be read by the use of a laser. The popular compact disc for music is an example.

lidar: an instrument for measuring distance by using light.

light-emitting diode (LED): a semi-conductor diode which emits light when an electric current is injected.

lithographic masks: masks with pre-determined patterns used in the process of making integrated circuits. For example a mask is used to define all the interconnections between the transistors.

macroscopic world: full-size world as opposed to microscopic world.

Magnetic Resonance Imaging (MRI): a way of getting pictures of internal organs of the body using magnetic resonance technique.

magneto-optic materials: materials whose optical properties are changed with the application of a magnetic field.

medium-scale integration: a semi-conductor circuit with may be up to hundreds of transistors.

metal-oxide-silicon: a transistor made by sandwiching a layer of oxide of silicon between silicon wafer and a metal layer. A very convenient way of making memory wafer chips.

microprocessor: the guts of a computer on a chip with a CPU, some memory and control circuits.

microwave: electromagnetic waves in the wavelength range of about 30 cm down to 1 cm.

NMR Tomography: another name for Magnetic Resonance Imaging (MRI).

MYCIN: an expert systems for medical diagnosis.

optical-fiber transmission system: an information transmission system using fiber optics.

oscillator: an electronic circuit that generates electrical power at an alternating frequency, usually to describe a radio frequency source.

passivation coating: an outer coating to make the surface non-reactive with the environment.

pattern-recognition unit: a machine that can recognize specific pictures or patterns.

pay-as-you-view services: a cable-TV service that offers movies for the viewers at a fixed fee.

photo-lithographic techniques: using light and masks to make patterns on semi-conductor wafers.

photo luminescence: a phenomenum of light emission from a material when the material is hit by a stream of electrons.

photo-refractive materials: a material whose refractive index is altered by the intensity of light shine on it.

photons: the particular representation of light in physics. A photon of certain mass is a wave packet of certain frequency.

point-contact diode: a junction diode with a point contact junction.

polyvinyl chloride (PVC): a polymer material of great versatility, used extensively as insulation jacket for electrical wires.

private branch exchange (PBX): telephone switch used in big offices where there are many extensions of telephones.

protective ozone layer: a layer of ozone in the upper atmosphere above the earth. It prevents the harmful ultra-violet light from the sun from reaching the earth surface.

Pulse Code Modulation (PCM): a way of coding information into on-off pulses. The practical realization in integrated circuits is the basis for the modern digital telephone system to meet its economic objective.

quantum mechanics: a branch of physics that explains mechanics of atomic scale particles.

Random Access Memories (RAM): semi-conductor memory chips that allow the stored information to be accessed randomly.

semi-conductors: materials such as silicon, germanium, gallium arsenide, for electronic device applications. They are neither an insulator nor a conductor but somewhat in between, hence the name semi-conductors.

silicon wafer: a slice of silicon single crystal material.

simplex method: a numerical computation method.

sub-atomic world: within the atom.

super-low-loss fibers: optical fibers with very high transparency. Light intensity falls by half after traveling along the fiber over a distance of 100 km.

Theory of Catalysis: catalysis is the science of chemical reactions induced by a catalyst, a substance which causes the reaction to take place but remain unchanged after the reaction has been completed.

Theory of Chaos: physics of random processes.

triode: a vacuum electronic tube with three electrodes, i.e. a cathode, a grid and an anode, used in amplifiers and oscillators.

turbo-charger: an after burner that boosts power output of a jet engine.

ultra-large-scale integration: a ULSI circuit is an integrated circuit with millions transistors on a wafer.

vacuum tubes: electronic devices having rectifying and amplifying characteristics.

very-large-scale integration: a VLSI circuit is an integrated circuit with around 100,000 transistors.

voice-activated dialing: telephone dialing by simply speaking the numbers, also known as voice-command dialing.

voice-recognition chip: a VLSI circuit capable of allowing speech recognition to be realized.

wafer-scale integration: a circuit integrated on the entire area of a semi-conductor wafer usually with many sub-circuits consisting of millions of transistors.